EXPERIENCE

LONDON

◉ Walking Eye App

Your Insight Guide now includes a free app and eBook, dedicated to your chosen destination, all included for the same great price as before. They are available to download from the free Walking Eye container app in the App Store and Google Play. Simply download the Walking Eye container app to access the eBook and app dedicated to your purchased book. The app features an up-to-date A to Z of travel tips, information on events, activities and destination highlights, as well as hotel, restaurant and bar listings. See below for more information and how to download.

MULTIPLE DESTINATIONS AVAILABLE

Now that you've bought this book you can download the accompanying destination app and eBook for free. Inside the Walking Eye container app, you'll also find a whole range of other Insight Guides destination apps and eBooks, all available for purchase.

DEDICATED SEARCH OPTIONS

Use the different sections to browse the places of interest by category or region, or simply use the 'Around me' function to find places of interest nearby. You can then save your selected restaurants, bars and activities to your Favourites or share them with friends using email, Twitter and Facebook.

FREQUENTLY UPDATED LISTINGS

Restaurants, bars and hotels change all the time. To ensure you get the most out of your guide, the app features all of our favourites, as well as the latest openings, and is updated regularly. Simply update your app when you receive a notification to access the most current listings available.

TRAVEL TIPS & DESTINATION OVERVIEWS

The app also includes a complete A to Z of handy travel tips on everything from visa regulations to local etiquette. Plus, you'll find destination overviews on shopping, sport, the arts, local events, health, activities and more.

HOW TO DOWNLOAD THE WALKING EYE

Available on purchase of this guide only.

1. Visit our website: www.insightguides.com/walkingeye
2. Download the Walking Eye container app to your smartphone (this will give you access to both the destination app and the eBook)
3. Select the scanning module in the Walking Eye container app
4. Scan the QR code on this page – you will be asked to enter a verification word from the book as proof of purchase
5. Download your free destination app* and eBook for travel information on the go

* Other destination apps and eBooks are available for purchase separately or are free with the purchase of the Insight Guide book

CONTENTS

LONDON
OVERVIEW

Ever since the Romans came, saw and expanded a small Saxon town on the banks of the Thames naming it Londinium, Britain's capital has excelled at changing and growing, two things it has not stopped doing for two millennia.

The English historian and scholar Edward Gibbon said of London in the 18th century: 'it is an astonishing and perpetual spectacle'. And, although it's no longer the biggest city in the world nor the centre of a huge British empire, London is still a vast and vibrant 24-hour show. A place where you can: watch buskers on the South Bank and groundbreaking theatre at the Donmar; see soldiers in bearskin hats performing ancient rituals in front of Buckingham Palace and inline skaters doing their exuberant thing to a hip hop beat in Hyde Park; view Victorian bustles in the V&A costume hall and a parade of the latest fashion tribes at Brick Lane market.

It is also no exaggeration to say it's a world in one city. London has always thrived on a continuous flow of immigrants who contribute in untold ways to its cultural life without changing its quintessentially British nature. Many of the Michelin stars now awarded to London chefs are not just for imaginative British cuisine, but also for masala dosas and dim sum. London may no longer be the world's most important port, but it has found other ways to be world-leading. The once run-down part of east London, Hoxton, has become a premier modern art market.

Where many cities are pickled in aspic, London keeps adding spectacular new buildings to its canon. The upstart London Eye has been going strong since 2000, having made a huge impact on how visitors view the city, both literally and figuratively. Along with other relative newcomers to the horizon – the Shard, the 'Gherkin', the 'Walkie Talkie' and Tate Modern with its new extension – it's made London a fun place again. And the exciting new venues, and regeneration for London 2012 Olympics, have further built on this new-found confidence and vibrancy. Enjoy!

IN THE MOOD FOR...

... STREET LIFE

Britons are widely regarded as being rather reserved, but British street life has always been very lively. And so it is that a city where everybody obediently stands to the right on the escalator is also the birthplace of punk and the cradle of wildly inventive designers like Vivienne Westwood, John Galliano and the late Alexander McQueen. If you want to observe the next flowering of British street style hang around **Seven Dials** (see page 60) where Central St Martins fashion students are to be seen rocking their latest creations, or **Brick Lane** (see page 113) where many fledgling designers are setting up new stalls and shops. Markets are also excellent for people/style-watching – try **Camden** (see page 155) for rocker types; **Portobello** (see page 154) for boho beauties, and **Broadway Market** (see page 157) for the art tribe. London also has great street art and performance. The tube has licensed buskers in 25 central stations, and during any walk on the **South Bank** (see page 128), you will be serenaded by musicians of every genre. Perhaps the best spot to watch London street life is outside **Bar Italia** (see page 48).

... FINE DINING

Britain is still behind France and Japan for Michelin stars, but London's constellation, which increases most years, has helped to establish and strengthen the country's reputation as a gastro *tour de force* – and Mayfair has the highest concentration of Michelin-starred restaurants in London. Take your pick (see page 34).

If you want to understand how traditional British cooking became great again, **St John** (see page 102) is the go-to place. There are few parts of the animal, from intestines to bone marrow, that haven't found their way onto a plate in this renowned restaurant. And at **Hix** (see page 50) you can see another chef (the eponymous Mark) in his prime reinventing classic British dishes such as meat pies or sand dabs and making them lighter, and more inventive and delicious, than they sound. At **Sketch** (see page 34) you can sample Michelin-starred cuisine in ornate surroundings, or top British cuisine from chef **Jason Atherton** (see page 34) in one of his restaurants. Innovative spicing and exquisite curries from across India reward the British love of Indian food with a very classy curry house at **Benares** (see page 34).

... RETAIL THERAPY

You cannot discuss shopping in London without mentioning the holy trinity of **Harrods** (see page 136), **Harvey Nichols** (see page 136) and **Selfridges** (see page 40). But there is so much more to London's shopping scene than department stores. It has several high streets – in **Marylebone** (see page 38), **Richmond** (see page 160) and **Islington** (see page 156) – that showcase the best of the British chains along with funkier little independent stores. Then there are the speciality areas such as **Borough** (see page 122)

for food, **Carnaby Street** (see page 51) for quirky boutiques, **Mount Street** (see page 35) for couture, **Denmark Street** for musical instruments, **Brick Lane** (see page 113) and **Portobello** (see page 154) for vintage, **Newburgh Street** (see page 51) for cutting-edge fashion, **Bermondsey** (see page 127) and **Islington** (see page 156) for antiques and **Savile Row** (see page 37) for bespoke suits. Plus a handsome smattering of one-of-a-kind, only-in-London shops such as **Fortnum & Mason** (see page 33), **Liberty** (see page 51), **Geo F. Trumper** (see page 36) and **James Smith & Sons** (see page 94). Markets, both open-air and covered, are also very important – thousands flock to **Spitalfields** (see page 111), **Camden** (see page 156) and **Broadway** (see page 157) every week in search of fresh foods and smart fashions. And museum shops have come a long way from the dusty postcard and mug days – the retail spaces of the **British Museum** (see page 88), the **British Library** (see page 86) and **Tate Modern** (see page 124) are particularly noteworthy for their range of books, jewellery and objets d'art that you would not encounter anywhere else. The **Science Museum** (see page 138) has a range of toys that knocks Hamleys into a cocked hat.

... A NIGHT ON THE TOWN

Whether you want to put a Shakespearean play, an experimental drama, a heavy metal or indie band, a Hollywood blockbuster or an opera as the central entertainment to your big night out, London will have it in abundance. Just for starters for the list above, you could go to: the **Globe** (see page 125), the **National Theatre** (see page 128), the **Barbican** (see page 108), **Donmar Warehouse** (see page 56), the **Almeida** (see page 156), **The Barfly** (see page 155), the **Curzon** (see page 41) or the **Royal Opera House** (see page 53). For a drink beforehand, try the bar in the **St Martin's Lane** (see page 69) or the atrium bar halfway up **The Shard** (see page 120). For a meal afterwards, walk into **Chinatown** (see page 55) for something quick, cheap and delicious, or go for the full after-theatre splendour of **The Ivy** (see page 58). Or for something somewhere in between try **Vinoteca** (53 Beak St; tel: 020 3544 7411), a casually stylish wine bar with sharing plates and a terrific wine list.

If it's a glamorous, no expenses spared night out you have in mind, why not precede dinner in a gastronomic temple (see page 9) with a cocktail at the **Coburg** (see page 42) or the rooftop **Radio Bar at ME Hotel** (336 The Strand; tel: 020 7395 3400)? Or keep it simple and low-key and while away an evening nursing a drink or two in a good old-fashioned boozer – or gastro-pub if you want some food to soak up the alcohol (see pages 31 and 50).

... ROMANCE

A heartstopping view is a prerequisite for any romantic interlude so start with a stroll by the Serpentine, the stretch of water that runs between Hyde Park and Kensington Gardens, and perhaps a meander through the lovely **Serpentine Gallery** (see page 144) sculpture garden. There is no place more romantic for lunch than **The Orangery** in Holland Park (see page 154) or you could go for one with a view at **Oblix** at The Shard (see page 121). Then a spot of sightseeing at **Westminster Abbey** (see page 77), the fairy-tale setting of the wedding of Prince William and Kate Middleton. Walk past the **Houses of Parliament** (see page 67) and cross Westminster Bridge to the **London Eye**, where the seriously romantic can get a capsule to themselves for around £380 (including Champagne, naturally). **Hakkasan** (see page 55) where dim sum is given the full glamour treatment is a very romantic setting for dinner. A glass of champagne with a hint of Parisian adventures at **St Pancras** (see page 84) would round things off nicely, and if you and your beloved are still awake in the wee small hours, watch the sun come up over the big city from **Parliament Hill** (see page 161).

... FAMILY FUN

Although formal restaurants might ask children to shush, children of all ages should have a fantastic time in the big smoke. Busy chain restaurants like **Ping Pong** on the South Bank (see page 128), or **Carluccio's** and **Pizza Express** all over town provide paper, puzzles and pencils to small diners. The **Museum of Childhood** (see page 158) and the **Natural History Museum** (see page 138) are obvious choices, but most of London's museums have activities for kids – the free apps and family events at **Tate Britain** (see page 70), Hands On desks at the **British Museum** (see page 88) and magic carpet story-telling for under 5s at the **National Gallery** (see page 66) are huge fun. The **Science Museum** (see page 138) with all its interactive exhibits is always a hit. London's parks are a godsend when they need a run around. Most have playgrounds, but the best outdoor play space by a mile is the **Diana Princess of Wales memorial playground** (see page 144). And if they've behaved themselves, treat them to ice cream from **Oddono's** (see page 137).

... A QUINTESSENTIAL LONDON EXPERIENCE

Ask what the quintessential London experience is, and you'll get as many answers as people you ask. It could be: a hearty breakfast 'try-up' at **Smith's of Smithfield** (see page 102); a dainty lunch in stately surrounds at **The Wallace Collection** (see page 30) or the **National Dining Rooms** at the National Gallery (see page 66); exploring the best of British art over the centuries at **Tate Britain** (see page 70); a walk in the rain, or a cheese and pickle sandwich on a park bench

gazing at the rose garden in **Regent's Park** (see page 155); or a ride to the West End in a black cab or a boat along the Thames to **Greenwich** (see page 162). Then again it is probably strolling through **Columbia Road flower market** (see page 111) or hearing that announcement on the tube 'Mind the gap' for the first time. No, hang on, it's a cocktail and dim sum at **Hakkasan** (see page 55). No, no, no, it's a warm pint at **The Coach and Horses** (see page 50) ...

... HISTORY

The river Thames is both the reason London was settled and an explanation of how it went on to become one of the world's largest and most influential cities. So, walking along its banks is a great way of tapping into the city's past. The **Museum of London** (see page 110) enables you to absorb more of this history in its galleries, and the best slices of living history are to be found at the **Imperial War Museum** (see page 131), the **Cabinet War Rooms** (see page 74) and the evocative **Dennis Severs House** (see page 112).

... A LAZY DAY

The deckchairs in London's parks are like mini hammocks in which to slouch, chill and watch the world go by. The **Electric Cinema** (see page 41) has sofas for two in the auditorium and a bar with sofas on which snacks can be brought to you. Or catch a movie at the **BFI** (see page 129) and recline in one of the leather sofas at Benugo afterwards. A Sunday roast dinner is a fine British tradition, as is the habit of taking root in an armchair with a newspaper and a drink – great locations for this include **The Spaniard's Inn** (see page 161), **Only Running Footman** (see page 31) and **The Garrison** (see page 127).

... BEING PAMPERED

Most of London's swisher hotels such as **Claridges** (49 Brook Street; tel. 020 7629 8860) or the **Soho Hotel** (4 Richmond Mews; tel. 020 7559 3000) have in-room massage, and the **Sanderson** (50 Berners Street; tel. 020 7300 1400), the **Berkeley** (see page 147), **Brown's** (33 Albemarle Street; tel. 020 7493 6020) and the **Mandarin Oriental** (66 Knightsbridge; tel. 020 7235 2000) all have spas where you can get lost on a cloud of fragrance and steam. Or just give your feet a treat and walk them to the pedicure room at **Fortnum & Mason** (see page 33). For organic beauty products, soothing therapies and remedies in a relaxed, hippyish atmosphere, go to **Neal's Yard** (see page 60).

... BEING SPORTY

London is full of parks and green spaces but when you are looking for routes to run, consider also the river and **canal tow paths** (Camden to Little Venice is a lovely stretch). For a more 'wilderness' run, head for **Richmond Park** (see page 160) or **Hampstead Heath** (see page 161) which also has natural, verdant pools for open-air swimming year round. Those with wheels can join inline skaters near the boathouse at the Serpentine in **Hyde Park** (see page 144), or go horse-riding along the famous Rotten Row, also in Hyde Park.

... ROYALTY

There are palaces with royal pomp and splendour aplenty in London, not
just Buckingham Palace, but the **Tower of London** (see page 109), **Kensington Palace** (see page 145) and **Banqueting House** (see page 73)
have all housed and feted crowned heads. You can walk down the aisle at
St Paul's (see page 105) and **Westminster Abbey** (see page 77) where
royals have wed (and some are laid to rest). Almost all of the big parks –
Hyde, Regent's and St James's – were royal hunting grounds, but the most
beautiful of these is the one with deer still roaming, at **Richmond** (see
page 160). However, house and garden aren't the only ways of channel-
ling royalty – you could shop like them too and become a patron of one of
the many shops with royal warrants (see page 33); you can even shop
at Rigby & Peller, official corsetieres to the Queen, just around the corner
from **Harrods** (see page 136).

... SOMETHING FREE

The well-known saying: 'the best things in life are free' is so true in London, and although it can be an expensive city, you could have a pretty good time for nothing. Here's how: all the national art galleries and museums are free (although they encourage donations). There are free lunchtime concerts in London churches such as **St James's Piccadilly** (see page 43) and **St Martin-in-the-Fields** (see page 69) and free foyer events almost every day in the **Southbank Centre** (see page 128). If you wander through **Borough Market** (see page 122) you will be amazed at how much free food you are invited to try. And to relive sporting glory, you can take a tour around the 560 acres of parkland at the **Queen Elizabeth Olympic Park** (see page 158).

... LITERARY INSPIRATIONS

The obvious place to seek literary associations is the **British Library** (see page 86) where modern authors can be seen researching, along with the work of thousands of others stretching back to William Blake's notebooks and beyond. In **Bloomsbury** and the **South Bank**, you can barely move without touching something once touched by Shakespeare (see page 125) or Dickens (see page 92). Or head for **Hampstead** (see page 161) once a magnet for writers and intellectuals, to pay tribute to Keats and Freud. Bibliophiles should not miss a visit to **Charing Cross Road**, the giant **Waterstone's** on Piccadilly (see page 43), or the Edwardian travel bookshop, **Daunt Books** (see page 39).

... MODERN ARCHITECTURE

The metropolis is best known as a repository of ancient buildings and grand old palaces, but it has many marvels of modern architecture. These include: **The Shard**, Western Europe's tallest building (see page 120), **Olympic Village** (see page 158), and its Aquatic Centre by the late Zaha Hadid, the **'Walkie Talkie'** and the verdant Sky Garden (see page 106), Sir Norman Foster's 30 St Mary Axe – better known as the **'Gherkin'** – and his **City Hall** by Tower Bridge, the **Millennium Bridge** and the much-loved **London Eye** (see page 123).

NEIGHBOURHOODS

The Thames wiggles through the centre of greater London, but it is at the bottom of central London. The only bit of London south of the Thames visited by millions of visitors is the South Bank. North of the river, London is divided into the two areas of Westminster and The City, representing the cultural and financial centres respectively.

Mayfair and Marylebone. Marylebone, defined by Oxford Street to the south and Marylebone Road to the north, is a discreet residential area of Edwardian apartment blocks with a delightful high street. Mayfair is bounded by Park Lane and Regent Street and bisected by Bond Street. It is London's most blue-blooded area peopled by the gentility and peppered with Michelin-starred restaurants, grand hotels, couture stores and classic shops.

Soho and Covent Garden. Soho and Covent Garden, with their abundance of shops, restaurants and theatres, are the twin hubs of tourist London, but if you step back from their overcrowded centres – Piccadilly Circus, Leicester Square, Oxford Street and Covent Garden Piazza – you are in the chic and lively heart of the West End.

Westminster and St James's. To many, Westminster and St James's are central London. Between them they have the highest concentration of iconic buildings – the Houses of Parliament, Big Ben, Westminster Abbey, 10 Downing Street, Buckingham Palace, Trafalgar Square – not to mention the National Galleries and St James's Park.

Bloomsbury, Holborn and King's Cross. Bloomsbury is best known for its literary connections. Once the home of Virginia Woolf, E.M. Forster and Britain's publishing houses, it is still a thriving cultural area thanks to the presence of the British Museum and University College London. Made up of Georgian terraces with beautiful green squares, Bloomsbury and Holborn are pleasingly quiet areas to explore. Once a grotty area, the arrival of the Eurostar terminal saw the renaissance of the King's Cross area.

City, Clerkenwell and Spitalfields. The City, or the Square Mile as it is also known, stands on the original settled area of London, and is now the financial district. Thus thrusting glass and steel bank headquarters nestle against centuries-old churches and pubs. The warehouses and print shops of old Clerkenwell are now the loft spaces, bars and clubs of its stylish new inhabitants. Dedicated fashion followers and bargain hunters flock east to the markets and boutiques of Spitalfields and Brick Lane.

The South Bank. The South Bank is the south side of the river between Tower and Westminster bridges. If you only had time for one slice of London sightseeing, make it this. Here in microcosm you have the best of London: fantastic food (Borough), art (Tate Modern), architecture (The Shard), theatre (Shakespeare's Globe and the National), music (Royal Festival Hall) and history (Tower Bridge).

Kensington and Chelsea. Kensington, Chelsea and Knightsbridge are the most traditional, least changing parts of the city. Largely residential, the quiet squares and immaculate terraced housing are civilised, genteel pockets broken up by the posh shopping streets of Knightsbridge and the Kings Road, and the museum mile of Brompton and Exhibition Roads.

Village London. London is not a homogeneous city. It is rather a chaotic patchwork of overlapping villages all of which have distinctly different characters – stylish Notting Hill, edgy Camden, cosmopolitan East End, easy Islington, arty Hoxton, intellectual Hampstead, scientific Greenwich and green Richmond – all merit a visit.

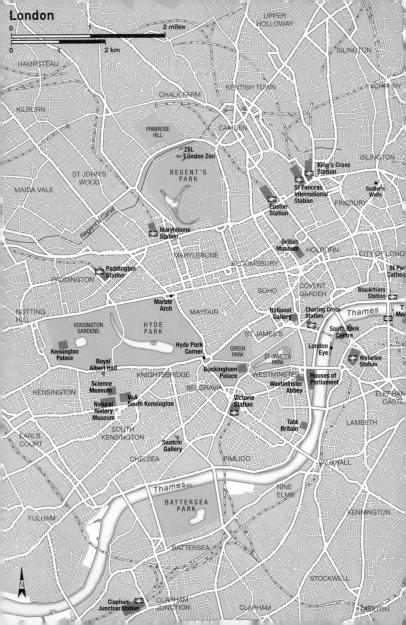

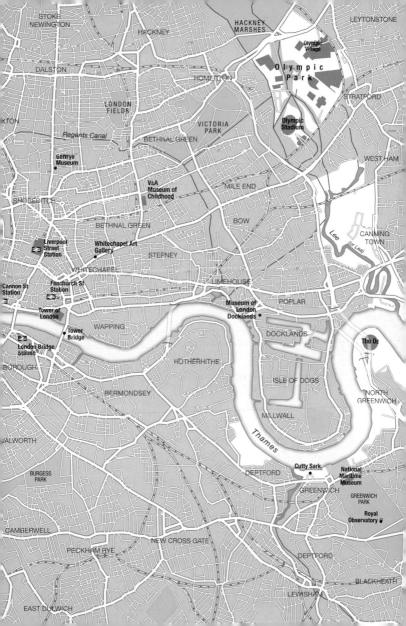

MAYFAIR AND MARYLEBONE

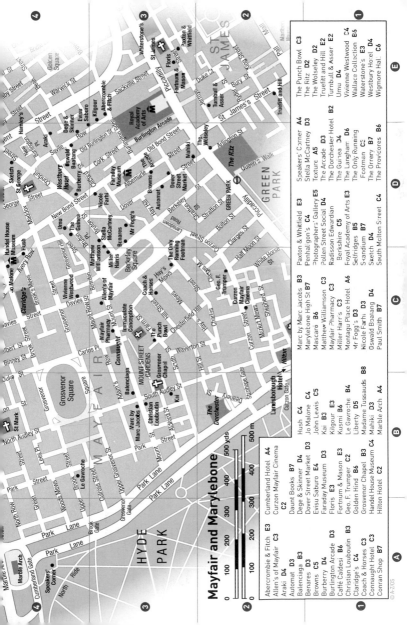

Mayfair and Marylebone

Abercrombie & Fitch	**E3**	
Allen's of Mayfair	**C3**	
Araki	**D4**	
Automat	**D3**	
Balenciaga	**B3**	
Benares	**D3**	
Browns	**C5**	
Burberry	**D4**	
Burlington Arcade	**D3**	
Caffè Caldesi	**B6**	
Christian Louboutin	**B3**	
Claridge's	**C4**	
Coach & Horses	**C3**	
Connaught Hotel	**C3**	
Conran Shop	**B7**	

Cumberland Hotel	**A4**	
Curzon Mayfair Cinema	**C2**	
Daunt Books	**B7**	
Dege & Skinner	**D4**	
Dover Street Market	**D3**	
Evisu Saburo	**E4**	
Faraday Museum	**D3**	
Floris	**E3**	
Fortnum & Mason	**E3**	
Geo. F. Trumper	**C2**	
Golden Hind	**B6**	
Grosvenor Chapel	**B3**	
Handel House Museum	**C4**	
Hilton Hotel	**C2**	

Hush	**C4**	
Jo Malone	**C4**	
Kai	**B3**	
Kilgour	**E3**	
Kusmi	**B6**	
Le Gavroche	**B4**	
Liberty	**D5**	
Madame Tussauds	**B8**	
Mahiki	**D3**	
Marble Arch	**A4**	

Marc by Marc Jacobs	**B3**	
Marylebone High St	**B7**	
Mascara	**B6**	
Matthew Williamson	**C3**	
Mayfair Pharmacy	**C3**	
Miller Harr's	**C3**	
Montagu Place Hotel	**A6**	
Mr Fogg's	**D3**	
Nicole Farhi	**D3**	
Oswald Boateng	**D4**	
Paul Smith	**B7**	

Paxton & Whitfield	**E3**	
Penhaligon's	**C4**	
Photographers' Gallery	**E5**	
Pollen Street Social	**D4**	
Radisson Edwardian		
Berkshire	**C5**	
Royal Academy of Arts	**E3**	
Selfridges	**B5**	
Scandium	**B7**	
Sketch	**D4**	
South Melton Street	**C4**	

Speakers' Corner	**A4**	
Stella McCartney	**D3**	
Texture	**A5**	
The Arcade	**D3**	
The Dorchester Hotel	**B2**	
The Guinea	**D4**	
The Langham	**D6**	
The Only Running		
Footman	**C3**	
The Orrery	**B7**	
The Provcores	**B6**	

The Punch Bowl	**C3**	
The Ritz	**D2**	
The Wolseley	**D2**	
Trufitt and Hill	**E2**	
Turnbull & Asser	**E2**	
Umu	**D4**	
Vivienne Westwood	**C4**	
Wallace Collection	**B6**	
Waterstone's	**E3**	
Westbury Hotel	**D4**	
Wigmore Hal	**C6**	

©A-ZGS

Breakfast in style at The Wolseley, a palatial café in the grand European tradition

Gone are the days when the only breakfast choices were a greasy fry-up in a working man's café or the bland buffet in big hotels. That has all changed and there's now a wide range of places in London providing seriously good options, whether it's an all-day breakfast in a homely pub or a decadent Sunday brunch. A fabulous choice to breakfast in style is **The Wolseley** – the renowned restaurant reviewer AA Gill even devoted a whole book to it, *Breakfast at The Wolseley*. It is a glimmering, shimmering place full of chandeliers, chinoiserie and old-world elegance, with an ambience more like a palace than a former car showroom (it was built in the 1920s by Wolseley Motor Company). Not surprisingly, it is an attractive – and very popular – place to have any meal, and magnet to the fashion, media, art and business crowds. There's an upmarket take on the full English breakfast, complete with bacon and black pudding. Or you could indulge in the classic Eggs Benedict, a touch of the colonial with kedgeree, or blow-out luxury with caviar omelette. For a healthy start there's also their classic porridge or muesli.

The Wolseley, 160 Piccadilly; tel: 020 7499 6996; Mon–Fri 7am–11.30pm, Sat & Sun 8am–11.30pm; www.thewolseley.com; map D2

Great places for breakfast

Apero (Ampersand Hotel, 2 Harringdon Rd; tel: 020 7591 4410), a bijou basement café near the museums; **Caravan** (1 Granary Square; tel: 020 7101 7661) for industrial chic in a converted grain store; **Chutney Mary** (73 St James's St; 020 7629 6688) for an unusual Indian breakfast in classic surroundings; **The Fox & Anchor** (115 Charterhouse St; 020 7250 1300) in Smithfield for a meaty breakfast with a Guinness; the **National Café** (see page 66) before hitting the gallery; **Polo Bar** (176 Bishopsgate; tel: 020 7283 4889) for a full English all day and all night; **Simpson's-in-the-Strand** (see page 58) for decadent surroundings; and the **York & Albany** (127–129 Parkway; tel: 020 7388 3344) for a hearty one before a walk in Regent's Park.

Go to a Sunday morning concert in the Art Deco splendour of the Wigmore Hall

Sunday mornings can be a dilemma when you are on a short break – it's Sunday so you want to take it easy, on the other hand, you are in an exciting big city with so much to experience. Attending a morning concert at the **Wigmore Hall**, held at 11.30am every Sunday, is a handy compromise. The concerts and recitals by a range of celebrated chamber music groups last an hour and there is a free glass of sherry or cup of coffee for all afterwards.

Originally called the Bechstein Hall, this concert hall is both impressive and intimate. It was built in 1910 by the German piano firm which had showrooms next door, but with the outbreak of war in 1914 came hostility to anything German-sounding and it was seized as enemy property. It was sold off for a song (to the nearby Debenhams Department Store) and reopened in 1917 as the Wigmore Hall. Thanks to its near-perfect acoustics, it has gone on to become one of the world's leading recital venues. Over the years many famous composers and musicians have performed here, from Arthur Rubinstein, Benjamin Britten and Jacqueline du Pré to András Schiff and Joshua Bell. There are regular events for children and special family concerts, and the restaurant and bar serves lunch and dinner daily.

The Wigmore Hall, 36 Wigmore St; tel: 020 7935 2141; www.wigmore-hall.org.uk; map C6

Take in superb works of 18th-century art set in an exquisite townhouse at the Wallace Collection

If you're on the verge of getting art or museum burnout, it might be time for a small gem of a museum like the **Wallace Collection** to revive your interests. The Wallace Collection is set in a stunning townhouse in tucked away Manchester Square, just yards from the teeming crowds of Oxford Street. It houses the personal collection of 17th- and 18th-century art, made by the Marquesses of Hertford and Sir

Richard Wallace, and bequeathed to the nation by his widow in the 19th century. It has been open free to the public ever since.

You will find a flurry of works to savour in the newly refurbished Great Gallery (now flooded with natural light): Old Master paintings such as Hals's *The Laughing Cavalier*, Rubens' *The Rainbow Landscape* and Velázquez's *The Lady with a Fan*. Elsewhere there are many other gems such as Louis XV's 18th-century commode, and a variety of Limoges enamels.

The Wallace is a beautiful formal space but not at all stuffy – kids love it especially when they head to the Conservation Gallery and try on one of the suits of armour; there's also a special children's audio guide.

Failing that, just go straight to the tranquil light-filled Courtyard Café in the atrium where you can have breakfast, lunch or afternoon tea, which should restore you to good spirits.

The Wallace Collection, Hertford House, Manchester Square; tel: 020 7563 9500; daily 10am–5pm; free; www.wallace collection.org; map B6

Prop up the bar and enjoy a pint of real ale in the lovely old-world boozers of Mayfair

Tucked away down a quaint little mews off Berkeley Square, **The Guinea** (30 Bruton Place; tel: 020 7409 1728; map D4) is a reminder of days gone by in a part of Mayfair that gleams with glass and steel modernity. Dating back to the 15th century, The Guinea is small, dark and atmospheric. It has Young's beer and excellent steak and kidney pies – plus the more formal Grill restaurant upstairs.

The Only Running Footman (5 Charles St; tel: 020 7499 2988; map C3) is a pretty pub that wouldn't look out of place on the edge of a village green. Its name recalls the time it was frequented by the footmen of the local Georgian aristocrats. Today the bar, mostly filled with a lively, mixed crowd, serves breakfast and Sunday roast. Upstairs the dining room is more elegant. The food is a cut above traditional pub food: Devon crevettes and rock oysters, bouillabaisse with sourdough, and slow roast pork belly. Desserts are very British, with apple crumble with crème anglaise and sticky toffee pudding.

Built in the 1730s, **The Punch-bowl** (41 Farm St; tel: 020 7493 6841; map C3) is the second-oldest pub in Mayfair, and once part-owned by film director Guy Ritchie, until he sold it in 2013. It's no longer the 'drinking venue to the stars', which some locals may rejoice about – it's now reverted to its life as a lovely old pub with bare floorboards, panelled walls and good locals ales, and a first-floor restaurant with a 1950s-inspired décor.

Thought to be Mayfair's oldest pub, the Grade II-listed **Coach & Horses** (5 Hill St; tel: 020 7355 1055; map C3) is pleasant and cosy – and although it doesn't boast sophisticated cuisine, it still serves a decent pint.

Take in a major exhibition then digest it over lunch or coffee at the Royal Academy of Arts

An abiding tradition of the **Royal Academy** is that whenever an artist is elected as a member, they are required to donate a work typical of their style. This amazing yet little-known collection includes bequests from Joshua Reynolds, Turner, Constable, Hockney and Tracey Emin. Highlights from the collection can be seen on free 1-hour tours (noon daily) of the John Madejski Fine Rooms.

But the Academy is best known for another of its founding principles, 'to mount an annual exhibition open to all artists of distinguished merit', which it has done every year since 1769. Now known as the Summer Exhibition (it runs from June to mid-August) it gets around 10,000 submissions a year from which the Academicians make their final pick of 1,200 works. And then there are the headline-grabbing showcase exhibitions such as 1997's Sensation featuring the YBAs (Young British Artists) that brought protestors and picketers along with throngs curious to see what all the fuss was about. Or the Anish Kapoor exhibition in 2009 in which a cannon shot red wax into a room of this beautiful old gallery at regular intervals. More recently, Ai Weiwei's hugely popular 2015 exhibition was captured in photorealistic stereoscopic 3D for online viewing.

After your gallery viewing there is thankfully a variety of wining and dining options to mull it over. There's the RA Grand Café, surrounded by Gilbert Spencer's murals, the bright, buzzy Atelier café in the foyer of their Burlington Gardens building, and in summer, the unbeatable Courtyard Café for a no-nonsense cup of coffee.

Royal Academy of Arts, Burlington House, Piccadilly; tel: 020 7300 8000; www.royal academy.org.uk; map E3

Be treated royally at Fortnum and Mason, the Queen's grocer

The Royal Warrants

Royal Warrants are a mark of recognition to companies that have supplied goods or services for at least five years for HM The Queen (or King). Mayfair and St James's have many shops with the royal warrant, including: raincoat manufacturer **Burberry** (21–23 New Bond St; map D4); bespoke tailors **Gieves & Hawkes** (1 Savile Row, map E3); cheesemongers **Paxton & Whitfield Ltd** (93 Jermyn St; map E3); shirtmaker **Turnbull & Asser** (71–72 Jermyn St; map E2); hatmakers **James Lock & Co Ltd** (6 St James's St; map E2); and bootmakers **John Lobb Ltd** (9 St James's St; map E2).

As you might imagine in a store where impeccably polite staff still wear tailcoats, its credentials are very impressive. In 1761 Charles Fortnum, grandson of the co-founder, went into the service of Queen Charlotte, winning it a Royal Warrant (see box) that is proudly displayed above the shop doors to this day. The store went on to become official suppliers of preserved foods to British Officers during the Napoleonic Wars, catered for state functions at the Court of Queen Victoria, and shipped beef tea to Florence Nightingale's hospitals during the Crimean War.

At around this time, Fortnum's (as it is commonly known) also began to supply luxury picnics to high society. These hampers became so popular that Charles Dickens wrote of a day at the races: 'Look where I will.... I see Fortnum & Mason. All the hampers fly wide open and the green downs burst into a blossom of lobster salad!' And it is still a very grand establishment, selling all kinds of delicate items from gentlemen's silk socks to slivers of smoked salmon. But despite this posh pedigree you can still find a jar of Marmite or mustard or tins of tea or toffees, and relatively cheap and quintessentially English items in this gleaming food hall.

Fortnum & Mason, 181 Piccadilly; tel: 020 7734 8040; www.fortnumandmason.com; map E3

Enjoy fine dining in the many-starred restaurants of Mayfair

Mayfair currently boasts 23 out of the city's total 65 Michelin-starred restaurants. Here is a list of edited highlights for your delectation:

If you want the 'grand French cuisine' experience opt for the three-starred **Alain Ducasse at the Dorchester** (Park Lane, tel: 020 7629 8866; map B2), the two-starred **Le Gavroche** (43 Upper Brook St; tel: 020 7408 0881; map B4), or **Hélène Darroze at the Connaught** (16 Carlos Place, tel: 020 7491 0668; pictured; map C3).

A place where it works to cheat by sitting at the bar (to still get the great views) is the modern European restaurant **Texture** (34 Portman

St; tel: 020 7224 0028; map A5). Lunches are often a better deal in these highly prized, highly priced places. **Sketch** (9 Conduit St; 020 7659 4500, map D4) prides itself not only on its two Michelin stars and superb modern global cuisine, but also on its décor: its main dining room, the Lecture Room, is completely redesigned every couple of years by prominent British artists – recent ones were David Shrigley and Martin Creed.

Proving that London's love of ethnic food can cut across all levels are **Kai** (65 South Audley St; tel: 0872 148 2277; map B3), considered the best Chinese restaurant in London, and **Benares** (12a Berkeley Square House; tel: 020 7629 8886; map D3) for classy contemporary takes on Indian cuisine. Recent awardees include **Umu** (14 Bruton Place; tel: 020 7499 8881; map D4) and **Araki** (12 New Burlington St; tel: 020 287 2481; map D4) both serving Japanese delicacies.

One of the nation's brightest stars, chef Jason Atherton has a total of eight restaurants in London. His first, **Pollen Street Social** (8–10 Pollen St; tel: 020 7290 7600; map D4) earned a Michelin star just six months after opening in 2011.

Discover the chicest little clutch of shops on Mount Street

Commence your fashion walk at the corner of South Audley Street and Mount Street, and you can nip into **Marc by Marc Jacobs** (24–25 Mount St) to have a look at the cute lipstick-shaped pens, colourful mesh bags and golden heart-shaped mirrors that they have for £1–3; it will be the last time you see a price tag like that for a while. On Mount Street, a beautifully preserved red-brick street in a quiet corner of Mayfair, you will find a cluster of some of fashion's most select names – **Balenciaga** (12), and **Christian Louboutin** (17) who said when he moved here in 2008: 'In this pretty street I want to have my prettiest shoes', and he's not let his fans down on that score. Next comes the **Marc Jacobs** couture store (24–25), and **Vivienne Westwood** is just around the corner (6 Davies St).

The other end of Mount Street seems to have been preserved in a Victorian bell jar. **Allen's of Mayfair** (117) is a 170-year-old butcher's shop – favoured by the many celebrity chefs in the locale – which was sold by its original owners in 2006.

If you need a secret hideaway after all that commerce, turn into Carlos Place and look for the discreet wrought-iron gated entrance to **Mount Street Gardens**. This is a public park, with London plane trees and ornamental shrubs, but as it's tucked away it's usually pretty quiet. For further respite, there's the **Church of the Immaculate Conception** in the southwest corner of the gardens. Built in 1849 for English Jesuits, it has a particularly lovely high altar by Pugin.

Mount Street; map B3–C3

Get a proper gentlemanly grooming at a very old-world hairdresser and perfumier

Just walking into this shop is a pleasurable experience redolent of history. The smell of eau de Cologne hangs in the air of this Mayfair institution, complete with mahogany panelled cubicles. **Geo. F. Trumper's** was established in 1875 and has been shaving the British elite ever since. And although it has gone on to become a globally recognised brand for the wet-shave enthusiast, the experience is pretty much unchanged. When you walk in you are greeted as Sir or Madam, and if you have a reservation for a cut or shave, the suited receptionist will phone down to the barbers waiting below to tell them to prepare the blades. It is allegedly here that Johnny Depp came to study shaving technique for his role in *Sweeney Todd*. Whether you're after a cut-throat experience – a 20-minute ritual starting with warm towels to

open the pores, and finishing with a discreet touch of moisturiser and a face massage – a quick beard trim, a pair of moustache trimmers, a badger shaving brush, or just a bottle of shaving lotion, Trumper's is the place.

Geo F Trumper, 9 Curzon St; tel: 020 7499 1850; map C2. Or 20 Jermyn St; tel: 020 7724 6553; www.trumpers.com; map E3

The uncommon scents of Mayfair

Other notable British purveyors of perfume and lotions in the area are: **Ormonde Jayne** (12 The Arcade, 28 Old Bond St; map D3), whose perfumier, Linda Pilkington, specialises in exotic scents; **Miller Harris** (21 Bruton St; map C3), where you can find modern takes on classic fragrances; **Jo Malone** (23 Brook St; map C4), for exotic combinations such as wild fig and cassis; and **Penhaligon's** (20A Brook St; map C4), for traditional and classic fragrances. Over in St James's, there is: **Floris** (18 Jermyn St; map E3), for goose-down powder puffs and single-flower fragrances such as Violet and Stephanotis; and **Truefitt & Hill** (71 St James's St; map E2), James Bond's barber, who also has a range of fragrances and products.

Be measured for exquisite tailoring, or buy off the peg, in Savile Row

The Japanese word for business suit, *sebiro*, is said to be a corruption of Savile Row, and this short street is synonymous worldwide with the artistry and craftsmanship of bespoke tailoring. Even the word 'bespoke' itself was coined here in the 19th century when a particular bolt of cloth was said to 'be spoken for' by a customer for his suit. The tailors here continue to make by hand what are widely considered the best suits in the world, and Savile Row has dressed European aristocracy and royalty, and every icon of male elegance from Nelson to Cary Grant to Jay-Z. A bespoke suit requires four to six fittings, takes five months to complete, and prices start from £3,000 for a two-piece. While the proud tradition of bespoke continues, there is around half the number of bespoke tailors in the Row than there were in the 1980s. The older established firms of the Row – **Henry Poole & Co** (15), **Dege & Skinner** (10), **Kilgour** (5), **H. Huntsman & Sons** (11) – have had to bow to the pressure of modern times and now also sell made-to-measure and even some off-the-peg ranges. And a newer, sharper modern type of tailor has moved in, as have menswear designers and brands like **Lanvin** (32). The new generation on the Row is represented by **Richard James** (29) and **Ozwald Boateng** (30) who, in their separate ways, have managed to infuse traditional tailoring with new colours and fabrics and 'sex up' the image of the Row. In the big building on the corner of Burlington Gardens is the flagship store of **Abercrombie & Fitch**, the American fashion brand. Its disco ambience and topless male models working as shop assistants have ruffled the sleek feathers of the old craftsmen of the Row.

Savile Row; map D4

Walk, look, stop, eat, drink and make well-chosen purchases down Marylebone High Street

Marylebone High Street has to be one of the world's loveliest shopping streets, a world away from the heaving masses of nearby Oxford Street. It is a near perfect mix of fashion, homeware, food and restaurants with a handful of charity shops where designer bargains can be bagged if you look carefully and time it right.

If you're there on a Saturday, the best way to experience Marylebone High Street is by starting at **Cabbages and Frocks** (every Saturday between 11am and 5pm) , in the grounds of St Marylebone Parish Church at the Baker Street (north-ern) end. It is a glorious combination of farmers' market, vintage clothing, cute handmade kids' clothes and homewares. There is also a food-only Sunday farmers' market.

The highlights as you walk down Marylebone High Street towards Oxford Street include:
Mascaró (13) for beautiful Spanish-made shoes and handbags.
Kusmi Tea (15) for classic and unusual tea infusions in elegant little tins, plus gift sets and glass teapots.
Paul Smith (38) which stocks the men's and women's shoe and accessory collections from the don of British fashion.

The Conran Shop (55), packed full of beautiful objects and textiles.

The Orrery (55) tel: 020 7616 8000) is a great French restaurant to meet for a relaxed lunch, plus a rooftop bar – a lovely spot to enjoy a Bellini on a warm evening.

KJ's Laundry (74) has super-stylish womenswear and accessories from designers such as Antigone and Catherine Weitzman.

Coco Momo Café Bar (79), a huge corner all-day café bar, is a good spot for a late breakfast of blueberry pancakes or early evening cheese board and a cocktail. There are a few outdoor tables –

great for people watching.

Brora (81) for very stylish Scottish cashmere in lovely shades, made at their own mill.

Daunt Books (83–84), with its long oak galleries and graceful skylights, is considered by many to be London's most beautiful bookshop. It specialises in travel literature and often has author speaking and signing events.

Skandium (86) for the best of Scandinavian homeware and furniture in a light-filled showroom.

Matches (87) designer clothing store with exciting young brands such as Thakoon, among the more established McQueen, Louboutin and Stella McCartney.

Kabiri (94) for eclectic, one-of-a-kind jewellery.

Caffè Caldesi (118; tel: 020 7487 0753) has a lively café-bar downstairs for antipasti and wine, and a more formal restaurant upstairs for classic Italian dishes.

The Providores (109; tel: 020 7935 6175) showcases the talents of New Zealand-born chef and owner Peter Gordon, while the ground-floor **Tapa Room** is great for all-day dining on innovative, lighter dishes.

Marylebone High St; map B6–7

Eat, drink and shop at a classic London department store

Selfridges is one of the busiest, and certainly the biggest, of Oxford Street's department stores, stocked to the rafters with great fashion and beauty. It celebrated its centenary in 2009, and there is even a TV series, *Mr Selfridge*, a period drama (2013–) depicting its glorious early days.

The nine-floor department store has a fabulous selection of mid-price high-street brands such as Jigsaw and Whistles, plus designer-store ranges like Joseph and coveted catwalk designers. Selfridges also boasts the world's biggest denim department – the Denim Studio, on level 3 – a dedicated 26,000 square-foot jeans haven with every style, from £11 to £11,000 a pair, from Primark to Christopher Kane. To accessorise your new togs, the Wonder Room showcases top jewellery and watch brands – a dazzling area dedicated to the most extravagant of luxury goods.

If you are hungry or thirsty there are plenty of in-store restaurants and bars to stoke up in. If London weather suits, there's the **Forest** rooftop restaurant and bar, with hearty hotpots, seasonal salads and cheeky cocktails. For something more cosy and decadent, the **Champagne & Oyster Bar**, in the food hall, has rock oysters from nearby shores (Jersey, Devon, Scotland and France), seafood platters and the best Beluga caviar. Newly refurbished, **The Brass Rail**, launched in 1966 and recently refurbished and reopened, is famed for its heritage salt beef bar – try the Reuben, hot salt beef with sauerkraut and Swiss cheese.

And if that gives you an appetite for more, you are well positioned to go and explore Selfridges' wonderful food hall.

Selfridges, 400 Oxford Street; tel: 0800 123 400; www.selfridges.com; map B5

Take in an arthouse film at London's longest-established independent cinema, the Curzon

Going strong since 1934, **Curzon Mayfair** is the dedicated cinephile's cinema *par excellence*. This two-screen arthouse cinema in a heritage listed building is a million miles from the multiplex experience: it shows live productions from New York's Metropolitan Opera and the Royal Opera House; is a venue for the London Film Festival; and has a long pedigree of showing independ-

The best cinemas in the capital

BFI Southbank (Belvedere Rd; www.bfi.org.uk; map page 116, B4) showcases films festivals and classic movies (see page 129). Launched by Catherine Deneuve in 1998, **Ciné Lumière** (Institut Français, 17 Queensberry Place; tel: 020 7871 3515) specialises in French-language films. **The Electric Cinema** (191 Portobello Rd; tel: 020 7908 9696) is London's oldest cinema, an Edwardian picture house with leather armchairs and two-seat sofas in the auditorium. Luxury hotels **One Aldwych** (map page 47, H4) and **The Charlotte Street Hotel** (15-17 Charlotte St; tel. 020 7806 2000) both provide 'dinner and a movie' deals in their plush mini-cinemas; **The Prince Charles** (7 Leicester Place; tel: 020 7494 3654; map page 46, D3) has regular sing-a-long showings, vintage films and all-nighters.

ent world cinema. It also wins prizes for a pleasurable viewing experience with its larger seats, wide auditorium, a four-seater royal box (which mere mortals can also enjoy), excellent sound, and raked seating to ensure you won't have anyone's head blocking your view. Here, you are less likely to encounter an audience chattering too loudly, or checking emails on their smartphones. This is vintage glamour.

The Curzon also has stage productions beamed in live from the National Theatre (see page 128), and themed double bills of old movies. The small bar is a lovely place to while away the time before your film starts.

The Curzon Mayfair, 38 Curzon St; tel: 0330 500 1331; www.curzoncinemas.com/mayfair; map C2

Enjoy glamorous cocktails in some very elegant bars

The Coburg Bar at the Connaught (see page 34; pictured; map C3) has to be one of London's most glamorous drinking places. The palette of jewel colours, the Julian Opie paintings, and the velvet wing-backed chairs make this a sumptuous setting to sink into while the bartenders expertly mix you an excellent drink. The cocktail menu boasts five varieties of a Manhattan alone, and there's a dazzling array of champagnes. Drinks are expensive, but complimentary little snacks such as perfect marinated olives and posh hand-cooked crisps soften the blow.

Meanwhile, **Polo Bar** (The Westbury Hotel, New Bond St; map D4) also avoids all the clichés of the hotel bar. It has splendid Art Deco fittings, a lively post-work crowd, flawless classic cocktails and elaborate bar food.

Hush (8 Lancashire Court; tel: 020 7659 1500; map C4) is another magical Mayfair location for drinks. The 'boudoir' bar on the first floor is perfect for an intimate drink, accompanied by the expertly-mixed cocktails – check the Bartender's Specials menu.

Mr Fogg's (15 Bruton Lane; tel: 020 7036 0608; map D3) is a quirky recreation of the fictional explorer Phileas Fogg's home, with dark wood bookcases lined with travel tomes, deep leather sofas and eclectic décor including a penny farthing hanging from the ceiling. Cocktails are suitably quirky and globally inspired.

Be uplifted by a beautiful little church with a big heart

Of the 52 churches that Sir Christopher Wren built in London, **St James's of Piccadilly** was his favourite. It is the only one not to have suffered damage during the Great Fire as it was safely away from the blaze on what were then the outskirts of the city. It wasn't so lucky nearly 300 years later, however, when London was under fire from bombs during the Blitz and it was badly damaged. Fortunately the font and organ case survived intact. They have very fine carvings by Grinling Gibbons, the Dutch-born sculptor who worked with Wren and Inigo Jones.

But this Grade I-listed church is better known for its inclusive attitude than its beauty. It has a little café in the garden which is a tranquil place for a coffee, and there are free lunchtime concerts (Mon, Wed and Fri at 1.10pm). Out front there is a bustling arts, crafts and antiques market (Mon–Sat). It is also the Centre for Health and Healing, and multifarious groups – from the Blake Society (honouring William Blake, who was baptised here) to the Zen Group – hold frequent meetings and lectures. St James's is also famous as a refuge for the homeless, and regular LBGT lunches. There is a caravan permanently situated in the churchyard where trained volunteers provide counselling for anybody in need of a sympathetic and confidential ear.

Just a few doors down towards Piccadilly Circus, refuge between the covers of a book can be found at what is arguably the best branch of the **Waterstone's** bookstore chain (203–206 Piccadilly). It has a bar and café on the 5th floor where you can enjoy international beers, European food and a cool view over South London.

Across the road is **Burlington Arcade**, the beautiful Victorian covered shopping street full of chic and interesting stores that are still policed by the quaintly uniformed Beadles.

St James's Church, 197 Piccadilly; tel: 020 7734 4511; www.st-james-piccadilly.org; map E3

SOHO AND COVENT GARDEN

1 Aldwych Hotel **H4**
100 Club **C5**
Aldwych Theatre **H4**
Baozi Inn **E3**
Bar Italia **D4**
Berwick Street Market **C4**
Bocca di Lupo **C3**
Boxfresh **E4**
Bridge of Aspiration **F4**
Busaba Eathai **C4**
Cambridge Circus **D4**
Centrepoint **D5**
Coco de Mer **E5**
Courtauld Institute **H3**
Courthouse Hotel **A4**
Covent Garden Hotel **E5**
Covent Garden Market **F4**
Donmar Warehouse **F4**
Fernandez & Wells **B4**
Fifi Wilson **E4**
Flat White **C4**
Foyles Books **D5**
Francis Edwards/Quinto **E4**
Freemasons' Hall **G5**
Gelupo **C3**

Gerrard Street **D3**
Hakkasan **D5**
Hamley's **A4**
Haozhan **D4**
Hazlitt's Hotel **D5**
Henry Pordes **E4**
Hix **B3**
Hummus Bros **C4**
I. Camisa **C4**
Ivy Market Grill **F3**
J Sheekey **E3**
Koenig Books **E4**
Koh Samui **E4**
Leicester Square **D3**
Leong's Legends **D4**
Liberty **A4**
Lina Stores **C4**
Little Lamb **D3**
London Coliseum **E3**
London Transport Museum **G4**
Masala Zone **B4**
Milk & Honey **B4**
Neal's Yard **E5**
Palace Theatre **D4**
Paul Smith **F4**

Pho **C5**
Photographers' Gallery **B5**
Piccadilly Circus **C3**
Ping Pong **B4**
Plum Valley **D3**
Polpetto **C4**
Polpo **B4**
Prince Edward Theatre **D4**
Princi **C4**
Ramen Seto **A4**
Rasa Sayang **D4**
Rock & Sole Plaice **F5**
Royal Opera House **G4**
Rules **F3**
Seven Dials **E4**
Simpson's-in-the-Strand **G3**
Soho Theatre **C5**
Somerset House **H3**

St Anne's **D4**
St Martin's Lane Hotel **E3**
St Paul **F3**
Stephen Jones Millinery **G5**
Superdry **E4**
Ted Baker **F4**
The Coach & Horses **D4**
The Dog & Duck **D4**
The French House **D4**
The Ivy **E4**
The Prince Charles Cinema **D3**
The Savoy **G3**
The Soho Hotel **C4**
Vasco & Piero **B5**
Wahaca **F3**
Waterloo Bridge **H2**
Yalla Yalla **C4**

© A-Z/OS

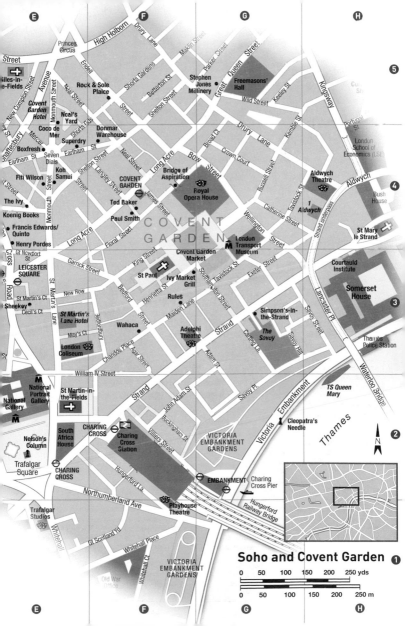

Soho and Covent Garden

Enjoy Italian delicacies and *ambiente* in and around Bar Italia on Frith Street

Soho was traditionally London's French quarter and the Italians were to the east in Clerkenwell, but due to road building and slum clearances at the outbreak of World War I, they started drifting west towards Soho; by 1934 it was regarded as more Italian than French. Soho is constantly updating itself, but many names from those days are still cheerfully dishing up pasta and pie with typical Latin flair to this day, including the celebrated **Vasco and Piero's Pavilion** (15 Poland St; tel: 020 7437 8774; map B5), a packed place with friendly service and classic dishes from Umbria, popular with politicians and designers alike. And two wonderful Italian delicatessens have survived all the renovations – **I. Camisa** (61 Old Compton St; map C4) which is small and busy, bursting with great meats, cheeses and olives, perfect for an impromptu picnic in any quiet little enclave such as **Soho Square** a block to the north or **St Anne's** churchyard on Wardour Street – and **Lina Stores** (18 Brewer Street; map C4) which hasn't changed since the 1930s and has a wide variety of delicious imported Italian goods.

Any self-respecting tour of Soho, however, should start, and finish, at **Bar Italia** (22 Frith Street; tel: 020 7437 4520; map D4). This almost-24-hour café (it closes from 5am to 7am) might not have the best espresso, but what it does have in spades is authentic Italian atmosphere and style. It also provides excellent people-watching from its small terrace. And if you choose to go on a night that the Italian football team is playing you will find it at its most characteristically colourful and noisy, as fans cram into the small back room to watch the game on the big screen.

Next door (21) is its posher sister restaurant, **Little Italy** (tel: 020 7734 4737), which is a little pricey but has very good, deceptively simple Italian food, and is favoured by Brit celebs – it frequently clears the floor for dancing after dinner.

Princi (135 Wardour Street; map C4) is the London outpost of Milan's artisan bakery and coffee house. And it has a similarly fashion-conscious crowd. It's a very smart marble-countered place, where the beautiful people gather post-work or pre-club for coffee and pastries or a glass of wine and a couple of shared *cros-*

tini. **Polpo** (41 Beak St; map B4) is a bustling, Venetian *bacaro* bar with lots of delicious tapas-sized portions of *cichetti* and *crostini*. It's new little sister **Polpetto** (11 Berwick St; map C4), a cosy spot with an *aperitivo* bar and open kitchen, also serves cichetti and more substantial dishes such as lamb *osso bucco* and rabbit pappardelle.

The lavishly praised **Bocca di Lupo** (12 Archer St; tel: 020 7734 2223; map C3) is a buzzy, lively place where the walls are hung with paintings by the chef's mother. And the menu has gathered together all the brilliant regional dishes – soups, pastas, risottos and roasts – of Italy into one enticing list. If you need another dessert or a late-night treat, visit its gelato shop **Gelupo** (7 Archer St; 020 7287 5555; map C3) with outstanding flavours.

Set off on a mini pub crawl of characterful Soho pubs starting at The French House

The French House (49 Dean St; map D4) once had a proper pub's name, but it became so widely known as 'The French' (rumours abound that it was the meeting place for the French Resistance in London during World War II) that the owners gave in and had a sign made up naming it officially. The drinking den of the poet Dylan Thomas and the painter Francis Bacon, The French still gets its fair share of bohos and old reprobates. If you yearn for a bar where the only sounds are conversation, this is the place to head – there's no music or TV, and mobile phones!

The Coach & Horses (29 Greek St; map D4) is much-favoured by writers and media types. This is partly due to the legendary Jeffrey Bernard, a journalist famed for his *Low Life* column in *Spectator* magazine, whose dedication to drink often rendered him unable to work, so the words 'Jeffrey Bernard is Unwell' would appear in place of his column: words that inspired a book and a play about him. It 2012 it became London's first – and probably only – vegetarian and vegan pub. A favourite is the 'tofu-ish and chips'.

The Dog & Duck (18 Bateman St; map D4) is an attractive Victorian pub – there was a time you could shoot snipe in Leicester Fields, now Leicester Square, hence the name. If packed, head upstairs to the George Orwell Room – he used to celebrate the launch of his books here. It's also served the likes of John Constable and Madonna.

If you have had your fill of pubs but not of drinking, go to **Milk & Honey** (61 Poland St; map B4) a stylish venue on three floors with great cocktails – reasonably priced for central London. It is a members-only club, but open to all earlier in the week if you make reservations (www.mlkhny.com).

Another cool bar to end your tour is **Mark's Bar**, the dimly-lit basement bar beneath the acclaimed restaurant **Hix Soho** (66 Brewer St; tel: 020 7292 3518; map B3), which has comfortable Chesterfield sofas and ever-changing cocktails.

Indulge in the mock-Tudor splendour of Liberty, London's most distinctive department store

The Newburgh quarter

Time was, Carnaby Street typified 'Swinging London'. Although those days are long gone, with many outlets for global brands, you can still find some independent gems in the New-burgh Quarter. Check out: **Peckham Rye** (11 Newburgh St) a small store crammed with rakish 1940s-inspired menswear; **Onitsuka Tiger** (15 New-burgh St) – the only UK outlet for this veteran Japanese brand of sneakers; **Chockywoccydoodah** (30 Foubert's Place), a chocolate 'boutique' with handcrafted sculptural creations and cakes; **Joy Everley** (7 Newburgh St) – quirky handcrafted jewellery from previous metals.

Liberty has always been strongly associated with the Arts and Crafts and Art Nouveau movements and continues to showcase new designers to this day, whether it is cutting-edge fashion by Christopher Kane, furniture by Vitra, or more routine items, such as bags, books, bikinis or bracelets. The striking exterior, with mock-Tudor beams, stretches along the whole block. The store was built in 1924, construct-ed from wood timbers from two ships, HMS *Impregnable* and HMS *Hindustand*. The lower ground floor has a beautifully laid-out menswear department, plus Murdock Barbers and grooming. There is also a stylish café, as strong on people-watching as it is for brunch and afternoon tea. The ground floor has beauty, jewellery – lots of lovely Art Deco pieces – accessories and the sump-tuous haven of the scarf hall with traditional Liberty prints, such as the famous ostrich-feather pattern alongside pieces by up-and-coming talents. Upstairs in the wood-pan-elled galleried rooms you will find an eclectic selection of womenswear.

Opposite Liberty's, you can take afternoon tea in the bijou **Court-house Hotel** (19–21 Great Marlbor-ough St; map A4), stylishly converted from the old Magistrates Court with many of the original features intact.

Liberty, 214–220 Regent St; tel: 020 7734 1234; www.liberty.co.uk; map A4

Eat your way round the world in and around Wardour Street

Hummus Bros (88 Wardour St; tel: 020 7734 1311; map C4) really know how to make a meal out of hummus. They send it out with plenty of hot pitta bread, pile on delicious toppings such as chicken or slow-cooked beef with caramelised onions, and offer lovely Mediterranean salads and side dishes to accompany. **Busaba Eathai** (106–110 Wardour St; tel: 020 7255 8686; map C4) might have a queue but is worth a wait for the flavour-packed, inexpensive Thai specials, with communal tables. **Pho** (163 Wardour St; tel: 020 7434 3938; map C5) is an easygoing Vietnamese café known best for its traditional rice noodle soup with fresh herbs – very

popular with diners on a gluten-free diet. **Masala Zone** (9 Marshall St; tel: 020 7287 9966; map B4) is a mini chain of colourful venues with original art on the walls, serving delicious, reasonably priced Indian street foods, such as *pau bhaji* – a pile of chilli-hot grilled vegetables in naan bread. **Ping Pong** (45 Great Marlborough St; tel: 020 7851 6969; pictured; map B4) is another chain – albeit a small and select one. They specialise in Chinese dumplings – dim sum – and give good advice to those uncertain of what to order.

Yalla Yalla (1 Greens Court; tel: 020 7287 7663; map C4) is a small hip café serving Beirut street food. **Rasa Sayang** (5 Macclesfield St; tel: 020 7734 1382; D4) is a no-frills venue with authentic one-dish meals from Malaysia and Singapore, most of which are well under a tenner.

If you want a coffee after – or were only ever interested in the caffeine course – proceed directly to **Fernandez & Wells** (73 Beak St; map B4) for what is widely said to be the best coffee in London, served from a stripped-down wooden counter. **Flat White** (17 Berwick St; map C4) is another good spot for coffee that makes it the way the Antipodeans like it.

Have a night at the Royal Opera House

There's more to this superb music venue than meets the eye. It's not just a world-class opera house, it is also home to The Royal Ballet and The Linbury Studio Theatre, where experimental dance and music are staged. Built in 1732, the four-tiered main auditorium was regilded and restored to former glory in 1999 – a suitably grand setting for world-famous tenors, divas and ballet dancers. To ensure that the performances are accessible to all, a range of cheap tickets is offered from as little as £8 – making it cheaper than going to the cinema. Even if classical entertainments are not your cup of tea, the 2.5-acre Opera House merits a visit. The centrepiece of the renovation is a soaring arched-glass atrium, and the **Amphitheatre Res-** **taurant** on the top floor is a spacey minimalist setting for light lunches and pre-opera meals. In warmer months grab a seat on its outdoor terrace which has fantastic views across Covent Garden Piazza.

Another way to appreciate how vast the Royal Opera House is, is to take a tour (there are various specific themes, running daily). Visitors are led backstage and often have a look inside the workshops that produce the scores of costumes required for each production. It's a fully working theatre so each tour is unique, depending if there are rehearsals at the time. You might be lucky and see the Royal Ballet in class.

Royal Opera House, Bow Street; tel: 020 7304 4000; www.roh.org.uk; map G4

See how British design guru Sir Paul Smith has turned Floral Street into menswear central

When Paul Smith bought his first shop – a dilapidated former bakery – on **Floral Street** in 1975, the entire area was a wasteland. The fruit and vegetable market had been closed down and its transformation into the Piazza shopping centre and tourist attraction wasn't completed until 1980. So when the first London Paul Smith store opened fashion hounds had to make a pilgrimage into Covent Garden for his 'classic with a twist' take on British menswear and eclectic collection of other objects and curiosities for sale. The original shop has expanded, and where Sir Paul (he was knighted in 2000) led, others have followed, making Floral Street an ideal location to browse menswear outfitters.

The **Paul Smith** emporium (40–44 Floral St) is four connected shops you can wander around, with men's and women's collections of dapper, essentially English, but not at all stuffy clothing, plus lots of accessories and trinkets in his signature stripes. One of the rising names in British menswear, **Nigel Hall** (18) is known for his sharply cut casual and smart-casual coats, suites and shirts. French designer **Agnès B** (35) has her understated, beautifully cut men's suits and leisure wear in the basement and on the ground floors, and **Ted Baker** (9–10) has good mid-price, good-quality, high-street fashion. A new kid on the block is **Orlebar Brown** (11), with men's resortwear and swimwear. Running parallel to Floral Street, Long Acre is home to **Jack Wills** (34), which is all about the British take on preppy – jersey tops and rugby shirts are a speciality.

Don't forget to look up when in Floral Street or you'll miss the 'Bridge of Aspiration', the ethereal glass and aluminium walkway that provides the dancers of the Royal Ballet School with a direct link to the Royal Opera House.

Floral Street; map F4

Sample dim sum, dumplings and duck in London's small but perfectly formed Chinatown

London's **Chinatown** may be small but what it lacks in size it makes up in colour and character. Also, it is on the doorstep of London's theatreland which, with its swiftly served, inexpensive food available all day and on into the small hours, makes it very convenient as part of a night out in the West End. In recent years some exciting restaurants have moved in to shake up the scene, and create a gastro buzz. The most notable are:

Haozhan (8 Gerrard St; tel: 020 7434 3838; map D4) has food from all over China as well as delightful European-influenced oddities such as Marmite prawns and coffee pork ribs. **Plum Valley** (20 Gerrard St; tel: 020 7494 4366; map D3) has excellent and adventurous dim sum at lunchtime, and a range of rice dishes cooked in a clay pot as an evening meal for two. **Leong's Legends** (4 Macclesfield St; tel: 020 7287 0288; map D4) is highly praised for its excellent spicy and garlicky Taiwanese food, though the service can be brusque. The atmospheric **Baozi Inn** (25 Newport Court; tel: 020 287 6877; map E3) is named after the savoury stuffed bun that is the ubiquitous snack of northern China; their version is top-notch, as is the rest of the Chengdu street food. **Little Lamb** (72 Shaftesbury Ave; tel: 020 7287 8078; map D3), an outpost of a mainland China chain, serves the best Mongolian hot pot. The title for London's best Chinese restaurant, however, most frequently goes to **Hakkasan** (8 Hanway Place; tel: 020 7907 1888, map C5), a sleek, sexy, very 'in' basement restaurant.

Take a seat at one of theatreland's most exciting 'little' theatres, the Donmar Warehouse

You can't judge a book by its cover or judge a play by its theatre. And yet, chances are if you pick a play put on by the **Donmar Warehouse**, you'll probably have picked a winner. It is only small – it seats 251 – but it is the most influential theatre in London, having staged productions that have gone on to receive 45 Olivier Awards (British theatre awards) and 20 Tony Awards (for Broadway productions) between them. Founded in the 1960s, down a cobbled street in a warehouse once used for ripening bananas, the Donmar housed the Royal Shakespeare Company in the 1970s, and all Britain's most innovative touring companies in the 1980s. Then in 1992 Sam Mendes took over as artistic director and began season after season of attention-getting theatre, much of which went on to transfer to the West End and Broadway. In 2002 Mendes left to become the renowned film director of *American Beauty*, *Revolutionary Road* and, later,

James Bond's *Spectre* and Michael Grandage took over. Amazingly, the Donmar's record for churning out award-winning productions – which have included *Frost/Nixon*, Jude Law's *Hamlet*, *Parade* and *Piaf* – has not faltered. Tickets are hard to come by, but worth planning ahead for. It is a subsidised theatre and they release a limited number of £10 tickets for Monday nights. It's not the most comfortable – the seats are upholstered benches – but its rough edges and limited size add to the intensity.

Donmar Warehouse, 41 Earlham St; tel: 0844 871 7624; www.donmarwarehouse. com; map F4

Pick of the Fringe
The **Donmar Warehouse**, the **Royal Court** (www.royalcourttheatre.com), the **Young Vic** (see page 130), the **Almeida** (see page 156) and the **Tricycle** in Kilburn (www.tricycle.co.uk) are the main outlets for new writing, which between them have pioneered many of London's most exciting recent productions. Lively pub theatres include the **King's Head** in Islington (see page 156), the **Gate** in Notting Hill (www.gatetheatre.co.uk) and the **Bush Theatre** in Shepherd's Bush (www.bushtheatre.co.uk).

Enjoy the cultural riches and open-air entertainments of Somerset House

Thanks to an ambitious refurbishment that began in 1997, **Somerset House** remains one of England's finest 18th-century buildings with its courtly square, 55 fountains, beautiful old gaslights and spacious terrace giving out on to the Thames. Former headquarters of the Inland Revenue, Somerset House now encompasses a university, a fine art museum, several restaurants and cafés, and an educational centre running workshops for adults and activities for children. Plus there's an exciting programme of open-air films and concerts in summer (June and July), and an ice rink in winter (November to January). Perhaps the best way to start to explore it is with a free tour. There are two types: the Old Palaces tour (Tue 12.45 & 2.15pm) and Historical Highlights (Thur 1.15pm & 2.45pm, Sat hourly 12.15pm–3.15pm).

The Courtauld Gallery in the North Building houses one of the world's finest private collections of European art from the Renaissance to the 20th century, best known for its superb collection of Impressionist and Post-Impressionist paintings including many famous ones by Monet, Manet, Van Gogh,

Gauguin, Degas and Cézanne. And there are a handful of more modern works by Modigliani, Matisse and Kandinsky.

There are plenty of eating options: **Spring**, the new 100-seater venue from Skye Gyngell, presents seasonal contemporary dishes in a bright setting; **Fernandez & Wells** for late breakfast and tapas in the East Wing; **Tom's Deli** is the latest venture from Tom Aikens with fresh British meats and comfort food classics; **The Courtauld Café** is for summer months, with tables spilling out onto the outdoor terrace – perfect for an afternoon coffee and watch the world go by.

Somerset House, Strand; tel: 020 7845 4600; www.somersethouse.org.uk; map H3

Dine with the establishment in the renowned traditional restaurants of Covent Garden

Thanks to its central location, **Covent Garden** has been London's first port of call for gourmands for three centuries. Between them, the following establishments have hosted most of the crowned heads of Europe and the most celebrated people of their day. For today's visitors, it's also a perfect neighbourhood for a pre- or post-theatre dinner.

Rules (35 Maiden Lane; tel: 020 7836 5314; map F3) opened in 1798 and claims to be London's oldest restaurant. It sources all its game from its own estate. While highly traditional, Rules has avoided becoming a museum piece and the dining room is beautifully atmospheric.

Simpson's-in-the-Strand (100 The Strand; tel: 020 7836 9112; map G3) is as much an institution as it is a restaurant. The 'bill of fare'

includes roast sirloin of beef that comes on a trolley under a huge silver dome and is carved just for you by an attentive waiter. **The Savoy Grill** (The Savoy Hotel, The Strand, map G3) was *the* place the establishment lunched. Churchill sat at table 4 every day; other fans include Frank Sinatra and Oscar Wilde. The hotel reopened in 2010 after a £220 million refurbishment and was restored to its 1920s Art Deco glory. The restaurant has likewise retained its excellence, with the likes of charcoal-grilled Chateaubriand.

The Ivy (1 West St; tel: 020 7836 4751; map E4) is theatreland's favourite dining establishment and a real celeb-magnet. The classics – Caesar salad, steak tartare and fish cakes – have near legendary status, but you have to book as far as a month in advance. Good news when the **Ivy Market Grill** (1 Henrietta St; tel: 020 3310 0200; map F3) opened then, which means visitors have more chance to taste similar dishes, albeit in a less formal setting.

For good quality seafood, **J. Sheekey** (28 St Martin's Court; tel: 020 7240 2565; map E3) is also a celeb haunt but it's likely that the chargrilled squid and Cornish fish stew will retain your attention even more.

Get to know an open secret at the Freemasons' Hall

Anybody who knows anything about the freemasons will know that it is a closed and very secretive society. And yet... they have left the door open to the public at their London HQ. The grand lodge was first built in 1775, as the city headquarters for what was then an occult order of men who believed that they had inherited a body of secret knowledge from before the Flood. That first building was deemed unsafe and the current hall, considered by many to be the finest Art Deco building in the country, was erected in 1932. And you are free to walk on in and get to know the freemasons of today through their library and museum – without the use of winks, nods or funny handshakes. There are free tours of this extraordinary building on the hour every hour from 11am

to 4pm on weekdays. It is worth it to see the Grand Temple alone; the massive, bronze doors open slowly out to reveal an enormous jade and marble chamber that can seat 1,700 and is magnificently, and mysteriously, decorated with the symbols and figures of Masonic ritual on panels of mosaic and stained glass. Photographic ID may be required.

On the same street (and named after it), **Great Queen Street** (32) is a busy gastropub, offering great modern British food with a lively Cellar Bar. Another noteworthy address on the street is **Stephen Jones Millinery** (36) which sells beautiful and eccentric hats for fashionable events.

Freemasons' Hall, 60 Great Queen St; tel: 020 7831 9811; www.ugle.org.uk; map G5

Find tranquillity and all things organic in Neal's Yard

Just behind the commercial madness of Covent Garden, **Neal's Yard** is a small quiet corner offering tranquillity on many levels. Benches and seats are scattered among brightly painted oil drums filled with unusual trees and plants. There are cafés upstairs and down, offering restorative cups of tea. And treatment rooms offer shiatsu, reflexology, a dose of Chinese herbal medicine, or a bottle of lavender oil to soothe your senses. When Nicholas Saunders, a 1970s hippy, opened his wholefood shop here, Neal's Yard wasn't even marked on the map, it was a rat-infested, squalid dump. But his shop was so successful that it led to a raft of world-renowned businesses including **Neal's Yard Remedies**, the organic beauty range, and **Neal's Yard Dairy** (17 Short Gardens), specialising in the then-uncelebrated British farm cheeses. **The Neal's Yard Therapy Rooms** (2 Neal's Yard; tel: 020 7379 7662) are an oasis of calm which you can use as a day spa or just book in for one treatment such as a facial or massage. Tortillas, Turkish meze and tandooris are among the delicious meat-free offerings from **Wild Food Café** (14 Neal's Yard).

Neal's Yard; map E5

Seven Dials

Neal's Yard is in the **Seven Dials** (www.sevendials.co.uk; map E4) area of Covent Garden, one of the hippest 'hidden villages' of the metropolis. Here you can find: **Coco de Mer** (23 Monmouth St), a sexy store concentrating on 'bedroom products' and all things sensual; **Hotel Chocolat School of Chocolat** (4 Monmouth St), the exquisite store with an aroma-filled café; **Orla Kiely** (31 Monmouth St) and her iconic graphic prints in clothing, homeware and bags; **Superdry** (Thomas Neal's Centre), the super-trendy casual brand.

Check out what's in focus now at the Photographers' Gallery

This is the largest public gallery in London (and the first in the world) dedicated to photography. It moved to its current location in 2012 (previously it was split over two adjacent venues in Great Newport Street). The **Photographers' Gallery** doesn't merely show emerging young photography talent, it fosters and encourages it with sponsorships, educational programmes and prizes, including the prestigious Deutsche Börse prize. Since its foundation in 1971, the Gallery has played an important role in establishing photography as a serious art form in the UK. To look at any one of their exhibitions is to become somewhat involved in the photographers' world – to see things their way a little bit.

The gallery has a reputation for exhibiting and selling the best of international photography of all genres – news, fashion, portraiture, art and the more experimental – in the past it's exhibited Capa, Salgado and Brandt, among others. And they have regular talks, screenings that either expand on current exhibitions or explore their archives, plus networking events. There's a first-floor **café**, and an excellent **bookshop** with an extensive range of prints and photography books including many rare or limited-edition ones. It also sells some secondhand photography equipment. The staff are informed and helpful, and the customers are a cool crowd who seem as much interested in hooking up with each other as they do in making purchases.

Photographers' Gallery, 16–18 Ramillies St; tel: 020 7087 9300; www.photonet.org. uk; map B5

WESTMINSTER AND ST JAMES'S

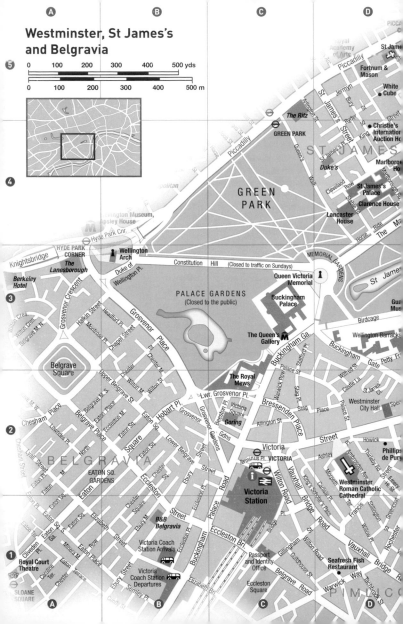

Westminster, St James's and Belgravia

5

0 100 200 300 400 500 yds

0 100 200 300 400 500 m

PICCA

Royal Academy of Arts

St Jame

Piccadilly

Fortnum & Mason

White Cube

Jermyn St

Bury St

Ryder St

King

St James's Street

Christie's Internatio Auction Ho

The Ritz

GREEN PARK

Arlington St

ST JAMES

Queen's Wk

Duke's

Marlboro Ho

Cleveland Row

St James's Palace

Clarence House

GREEN PARK

Marlborough

Lancaster House

The Ma

Horse

Ride

The

MEMORIAL GARDENS

MEMORIAL

St Jame

Wellington Museum, psley House

Hyde Park Cnr.

HYDE PARK CORNER

Knightsbridge

The Lanesborough

Wellington Arch

Duke of Wellington Pl.

Constitution Hill (Closed to traffic on Sundays)

Queen Victoria Memorial

i

Berkeley Hotel

3

Grosvenor Crescent

Wilton Cres.

Wilton Cres. M.

Belgrave M. N.

Halkin Street

Headfort Pl.

Montrose Pl.

Chapel Street

Grosvenor Place

St Chester M.

Wilton M.

PALACE GARDENS
(Closed to the public)

Buckingham Palace

Birdcage

Buckingham Ga.

Stanhope Row

Buckingham Gate

Wellington Barracks

Gua Mus

Petty Fr

Belgrave Square

Upper Belgrave St

Wilton M.

The Queen's Gallery

M

Wilfreds St

Castle La.

St James Palace St

Westminster City Hall

Spen

2

Chesham Place

Lyall Street

Lowndes Pl.

Belgrave Place

Eaton Place

North

Eaton Square

Chester M.

Wilton Row

Eaton M.

Eaton M. W.

Hobart Pl.

Grosvenor

Lower Belgrave Street

The Royal Mews

Lwr. Grosvenor Pl.

Bressenden Place

Grosvenor Gdns

Beeston Pl.

Victoria Square

Goring

Allington St

Place

BELGRAVIA

EATON SQ. GARDENS

Chesham Street

Eaton Pl.

Eaton Sq.

Eccleston

Chester Square

Ebury

Eaton

Street

Street

Victoria

Terminus Pl.

VICTORIA

Victoria

Palace Road

Vauxhall Bridge Road

Wilton Road

Street

Ashley

King's Scholars Pass.

Howick

Thirleby Rd

Ambrosden

Morpeth

Carlisle Pl.

Phillips de Pur

Westminster Roman Catholic Cathedral

1

Royal Court Theatre

Cliveden Pl.

Caroline Ter.

Eaton Ter.

Eaton Sq.

Chester Row

Minera M.

Eaton Pl.

Elizabeth Street

Ebury

Eccleston Square

Chester Square

B&B Belgravia

Ebury Street

Buckingham

Eccleston Brh

Palace Road

Bridge

Gillingham St

Guildhouse St

Belgrave Road

Vauxhall

Bridge

Francis

Stillington

Greencoat

Rochester

SLOANE SQUARE

Semley Pl.

Victoria Coach Station Arrivals

Victoria Coach Station Departures

Cundy St

Elizabeth Br.

Passport and Identity Office

Eccleston Square

Warwick Way

Tachbrook S

PIMLICO

Seafresh Fish Restaurant

Victoria Station

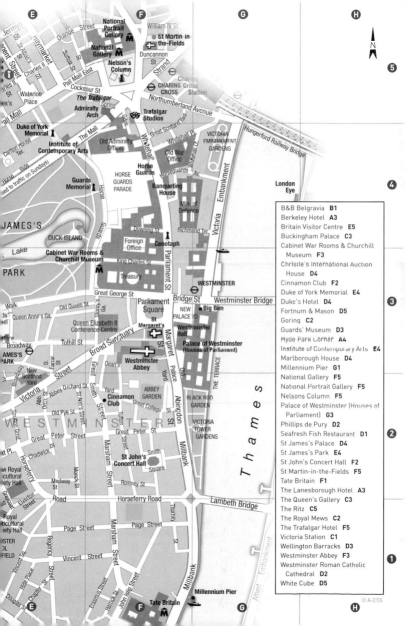

B&B Belgravia **B1**
Berkeley Hotel **A3**
Britain Visitor Centre **E5**
Buckingham Palace **C3**
Cabinet War Rooms & Churchill Museum **D4**
Christie's International Auction House **D4**
Cinnamon Club **F2**
Duke of York Memorial **E4**
Duke's Hotel **D4**
Fortnum & Mason **D5**
Goring **C2**
Guards' Museum **D3**
Hyde Park Corner **A4**
Institute of Contemporary Arts **E4**
Marlborough House **D4**
Millennium Pier **G1**
National Gallery **F5**
National Portrait Gallery **F5**
Nelsons Column **F5**
Palace of Westminster (Houses of Parliament) **G3**
Phillips de Pury **D2**
Seafresh Fish Restaurant **D1**
St James's Palace **D4**
St James's Park **E4**
St John's Concert Hall **F2**
St Martin-in-the-Fields **F5**
Tate Britain **F1**
The Lanesborough Hotel **A3**
The Queen's Gallery **C3**
The Ritz **C5**
The Royal Mews **C2**
The Trafalgar Hotel **F5**
Victoria Station **C1**
Wellington Barracks **D3**
Westminster Abbey **F3**
Westminster Roman Catholic Cathedral **D2**
White Cube **D5**

© A-Z/OS

Have a late night at the National Gallery

Friday Lates are a fun, cultural way to start any weekend in London. The **National Gallery** stays open until 9pm every Friday and you can wander about at will or stop and listen to live music, attend a lecture, join a 'walk and draw' group, have a drink at the bar or a snack in the café. The **National Café** is a good place to sit and plot your route – with more than 2,300 works in the collection, you'd do well to streamline your visit – and it's open until 11pm on Friday and Saturdays. The more formal **National Dining Rooms** is excellent for chewing over what you've seen over dinner.

The modern Sainsbury Wing contains the earliest works – mostly Italian paintings by old masters such as Giotto and Piero della Francesca, and holds the major temporary exhibitions. In the West Wing are Italian Renaissance masterpieces by Correggio, Titian and Raphael, and the North Wing has the 17th-century Dutch, Flemish, Italian and Spanish old masters. The gallery's most popular paintings are in the East Wing. These are largely works by the French Impressionists and post-Impressionists, including one of Monet's water-lily paintings and one of Van Gogh's sunflowers.

If you have kids in tow, there are fantastic family activities at the weekends including the 30-minute magic carpet storytelling sessions for under-5s (Sundays 11.30am & 12.30pm), painting or sculpture workshops for older children, and kids' audio guides and printed trails.

National Gallery, Trafalgar Square; tel: 020 7747 2885; www.nationalgallery.org. uk; daily 10am–6pm, Fri until 9pm; free entrance and free guided tours; ticket for major exhibitions; map F5

Study the many faces of Britain at the National Portrait Gallery

The original idea behind the **National Portrait Gallery** was to pay tribute to the nation's great men and women – all the people, celebrated or relatively unsung, who had contributed to the nation's history. And it is useful now to treat this grand old gallery as a collection of people and faces rather than of art. This somehow makes it less stuffy.

So, who are you interested in? The gallery's first purchase was the 'Chandos' portrait, widely believed to be of William Shakespeare, which could be used as a starting point for a tour of British literary greats. If royalty is your motivator, the Portrait Gallery has a photograph of Queen Victoria with her grandchildren, taken in 1900. There are plenty more portrayals of stiff-backed royals in paintings and photos, including the first double portrait of the Princes William and Harry in the dress uniform of the Household Cavalry. For a more informal contemporary royal, head to Room 39 for a sunny painting of the Duchess of Cambridge (aka Kate Middleton). You can find photos of 20th-century British heroes, from the late Mo Mowlam to Alan Bennett and JK Rowling.

The **Portrait Café** in the basement is a fun place for a quick

break, and the **Portrait Restaurant** on the rooftop is a fashionable foodie destination with wonderful views of Trafalgar Square, Big Ben and the Houses of Parliament. You can have a glass of prosecco at the Late Shift Bar, on Thursday and Friday late-night opening until 8.30pm. The bookshop in the main hall has a wide range of specialist publications, with occasional author signing events.

The National Portrait Gallery, St Martin's Place; tel: 020 7306 0055; www.npg.org.uk; daily 10am–6pm, Thur and Fri until 9pm; free; map F5

Hire a deckchair and admire the ducks, geese and passing civil servants in St James's Park

St James's Park is home to 15 species of waterfowl, including pelicans that have been here since the Russian Ambassador presented them to Charles II in 1664. They are not actually the same ones, of course, but the tradition continues and the Russian ambassador presents two to the court as and when necessary. The Park currently has four. Feeding time (they are given 12lbs of fish a day) is at 2.30pm. There are also ducks, geese, swans, moorhen, coots and grebe who nest here. This is amazing as grebe are very shy birds and St James's is one of the most popular parks in Europe with almost six million visitors a year.

St James's is the most romantic of the Royal Parks, with its crisscrossing paths, delicate bridge and weeping willows. So it is strange to think that in medieval times this was a soggy swamp where female lepers from the nearby St James's Hospice came to feed their pigs. It was Henry VIII who bought the land and made it into a deer park, but Charles II who landscaped it and opened it to the public. Find a bench or hire a green-and-white-striped deckchair and admire the view, which takes in Buckingham Palace, Big Ben, the London Eye, and the rear view of Whitehall and 10 Downing Street. This affords some excellent people-watching as the path that borders the eastern side of St James's Park is often filled with ministers and civil servants scurrying between meetings. Bring a picnic, or there's a restaurant, **Inn the Park**, open for all-day refreshments, plus four coffee and snack stalls.

St James's Park; map D–E 3–4.

Attend a candlelit concert at St Martin-in-the-Fields

Built in 1724, **St Martin-in-the-Fields** is the oldest building on Trafalgar Square. A church has stood on this site since the 13th century when the area was fields between the cities of London and Westminster. Ever since the turn of the 20th century, St Martin-in-the-Fields has wanted to be known as 'the church with the ever-open door'. The doors actually open just before 8am for the morning service, but there is something here for everyone right until the doors close after the evening concert at midnight. Even when the doors are not literally open, St Martin's is reaching out in some way, including working for the homeless. It was the first London church to allow a radio broadcast on its premises in 1924, for a Christmas appeal, and still broadcasts one annually on BBC Radio 4 which raises more than £500,000 a year for people in need. Because of its position next to the South African High Commission, the church became involved in the campaign to free Nelson Mandela and in the founding of Amnesty International, and the homeless charities Shelter and the Big Issue. It also has strong links with the local Chinese community, and has services in Cantonese and Mandarin on Sundays.

St Martin's is best enjoyed at dusk when the candles in the chandeliers are lit, and the elegant nave fills with music. It is a magical scene; and the evening recitals are of a consistently high quality. It is music that St Martin's is really famous for. The house orchestra, the Academy of St Martin-in-the-Fields, founded in the 1950s, has played an important part in the modern British revival of Baroque music, with regular recitals. The **Café in the Crypt** is a good place to stop for food, and there are also weekly jazz nights here on Wednesdays.

St Martin-in-the-Fields, Saint Martin's Place; tel: 020 7766 1100; www.stmartin-in-the-fields.org; map F5

Navigate the London landscapes and dine among a glorious mural at Tate Britain

Tate Britain was known simply as The Tate, until the Tate Modern opened across the river to give it some serious competition. But it would be a mistake to leave the quieter, older Tate sister out of any art tour of London. Holding the national collection of British art from 1500 to today, there is some seriously exciting, not to mention controversial, stuff here. Over the years this has included: Sarah Lucas's 2006 Christmas tree decorated with near-pornographic cherubs equipped with impressive genitalia; Martin Creed's installation, Work No. 850, saw an athlete sprint the length of the gallery every 30 seconds in 2008; and Chris Offili's retrospective, including some of his works decorated in elephant dung, in 2010. It also hosts the always-talked-about Turner Prize on alternate (even-numbered) years. But whatever attention-grabbing exhibition is on during your visit, it is worth making a quick tour of Tate Britain's London landscapes. These include: Turner's *The Thames Above Waterloo Bridge*, *State Britain* by Mark Wallinger, *Shelterers in the Tube* by Henry Moore, and two Constables *Kensington Gravel Pits*, and *A Bank on Hampstead Heath*.

The **Rex Whistler** restaurant is named after its huge, specially commissioned mural fantasy, *The Expedition in Pursuit of Rare Meats*, by Rex Whistler (1927). It features English pastoral scenes, tropical jungles and Rome's ancient chariots – a memorable setting for a meal. And the food and wine list are pretty good too.

Tate Britain, Millbank; tel: 020 7887 8888; www.tate.org.uk; daily 10am–6pm; free; map F1

Sit back on a boat trip on the Thames from Millbank Millennium Pier

The **Millbank Millennium Pier** is the most recent pier in central London to open and the most garlanded; a battleship-grey streamlined structure, it has won many architectural, design and engineering prizes. Due to its proximity to Tate Britain, the artist Angela Bulloch was commissioned to create a work for the pier, and transformed the entire structure into an artwork, by adding a light installation, 'Flash and Tidal'. Yellow and blue lights glow along the decks, alternating between high and low tide, while 63 programmed white lights flash on and off. Due to the changes of level at this point in the river – it can rise or fall up to 6m/20ft depending on the tides – the pier is moored quite far out in the river. You reach it by a long angled walkway and stand waiting for your river ride in what feels like the middle of the Thames. Seagulls wheel above your head, the waves lap – you have already escaped the city's frantic rhythm and you haven't even boarded a vessel yet.

If you are here following a visit to Tate Modern and want to visit Tate Britain, hop on the Tate Boat for the 18-minute journey to Bankside Pier. Or take the opportunity to see more of the city by boat and opt for a longer journey or a full city cruise – these range from hop-on hop-off City Cruises to the sleek Thames Clippers catamarans (used also by commuters). It is a great way of cramming in the sights for those who have limited time or who want to avoid traffic of the vehicular or touristy kind. Many companies run cruises and ferries from the pier (check the pier's website for details), which include trips with a guided commentary, and those with lunch, dinner, drinks or live entertainment.

The Millbank Millennium Pier, Millbank; www.millbankpier.co.uk; map F1–G1

Explore the White Cube, an ultramodern gallery, in old-world St James's

If you walk down Duke Street, with its many fine Georgian houses, and peer down a dark little alley, you'll be in for a surprise. For in the middle of Mason's Yard stands a stark grey-and-white oblong box. It looks as though it has been dropped there by aliens, but is in fact the **White Cube** – the gallery that is home to Lucien Freud, Chuck Close, Damien Hirst, Tracey Emin, Gilbert and George and Antony Gormley. It opened in 2006, around the corner to the original White Cube gallery – which was, as its name suggest, a small white box-shaped structure. (In 2011, a largest White Cube opened in Bermondsey.) Built on the site of an electricity substation, this White Cube is the first free-standing structure to be built in the St James's area in more than 30 years. The 1110 sq m/11,950 sq ft space hosts two major galleries – the ground-floor space is crowned by a glass lightbox, and a naturally-lit basement space. White Cube is a commercial gallery, owned by prominent contemporary art dealer Jay Joplin, but the public is welcome and its stated purpose is to 'stage something dramatic'.

More contemporary art

Surprisingly for an area with such tradition and grace, St James's has strong links with contemporary art. Here are some other places to explore this ironic juxtaposition. **ICA** (The Mall; tel: 020 7930 3647; www.ica.org.uk; map E4) is housed in a grand Nash building on the processional avenue. Inside they hold temporary exhibitions plus DJ nights in the lively bar, an art-house cinema, lectures, concerts and innovative installations. **Chris Beetles Gallery** (8–10 Ryder St; tel: 020 7839 7551; map D5) has a wide range of exhibitions, changing monthly, including contemporary photography and paintings; **Bernard Jacobson** (28 Duke Street St James's; tel: 020 7734 3431; map D5) is a commercial gallery with regular exhibitions by modern masters, and is also a major player in international art fairs and **Grosvenor Gallery** (32 St James's St; tel: 020 7484 7979; map D5) specialises in contemporary Indian art.

White Cube, 25–26 Mason's Yard; tel: 020 7930 5373; www.whitecube.com; Tue–Sat 10am–6pm; map D5

Gaze up to the most celestial ceilings in London at the Banqueting House

In a typically immodest claim, Flemish artist Peter Paul Rubens declared: 'My talent is such that no undertaking, however vast in size or diversified in subject, has ever surpassed my courage.' His courage may well have been tested by the commission to decorate the ceiling of the **Banqueting House**. Rubens was asked in 1634, by Charles I, to paint three massive canvases (two measuring 9 x 6m/30 x 20ft and one of 13 x 3m/43 x 10ft). The theme was to illustrate the wisdom and virtue of Charles's father, James I. The resulting canvases are the only ones by any important 17th century artist that are still in position in the place they were intended for. And they are magnificent to behold – the crowning glory of this beautiful Inigo Jones building that James I had put up in 1619 as the place in which he could entertain foreign ambassadors. It was the site of splendid court balls and dinners, and remains a place of entertainment to this day, hosting corporate events, fashion shows and wedding receptions. It is still also occasionally used by the Queen for banquets; she famously entertained George Bush here in 2003, causing anti-war protestors to gather at the gates. But, while entertaining has always been its bread and butter, the Banqueting House is best known in the history books for a rather grim occasion – the execution of Charles I. He walked through a window out onto a wooden scaffold in front of it in 1649. More happily, on the ground floor is the magnificent vaulted Undercroft where Charles II had raucous drinking parties. The Banqueting House is frequently closed for events, so check for closures before planning a visit.

The Banqueting House, Whitehall; tel: 020 3166 6000; www.hrp.org.uk; Mon–Sat 10am–5pm; map F4

Feel history come to life in the Cabinet War Rooms, Churchill's wartime bunker

London, it's a cliché to say, is full of history. But there is nowhere quite so perfectly frozen in time as the **Cabinet War Rooms**. In 1938, with war threatening, the basement of this Whitehall building was chosen as the Cabinet War Rooms – a shelter for the heart of government and military command. Over the next six years, hundreds of men and women, civilian and uniformed, spent thousands of vital hours working – and sleeping – in this maze of interlocking, underground rooms. The slightly claustrophobic chambers and the narrow corridors leading to them are in the exact same condition they were left in when locked up at the end of hostilities in 1945. In the Map Room you can trace the position of Allied forces as they triumphed on VJ Day. The pencils are still neatly placed by the notepads on the Cabinet Room table, and the public safety posters warning 'walls have ears' or beseeching you to 'keep calm and carry on' are still pinned to the noticeboards. You can almost hear the clackety clack of the typing pool and imagine the *basso profondo* of 'Winnie' practising his speeches to rally the nation as you walk through these 30, once top-secret, rooms. Stop at the **Switch Room Café**, halfway round, for tea, cake and sandwiches.

Churchill Museum & Cabinet War Rooms, Clive Steps, King Charles St; tel: 020 7930 6961; www.iwm.org.uk; daily 9.30am–6pm; map F3

Grace the royal apartments at Buckingham Palace

When the Queen packs her bags and goes off to her Scottish castle, Balmoral, for her summer holidays, Joe Public is invited in to her London residence to have a nose around. **Buckingham Palace** has 775 rooms – including 52 bedrooms, 188 staff bedrooms, 92 offices and 78 bathrooms. Only the state rooms are open to visitors in August and September (it is advisable to book ahead – and your ticket can be converted into a one-year pass). But they are the grandest of them all and do not disappoint with their glittering vistas of marble and gold leaf, walls liberally plastered with masterpieces by Rembrandt, Rubens and Canaletto, and the massive twinkling chandeliers on high. Highlights are the theatrical **Throne Room**, with the 1953 coronation throne, **The Ballroom**, where you can admire the sword the Queen uses to knight people, **The Music Room** featuring lapis lazuli columns between arched floor-to-ceiling windows, and the alabaster-and-gold plasterwork of **The White Drawing Room**. There is also a themed special exhibition each year.

The Queen's Gallery was built by the Queen in 1962 to allow the public year-round access to the Royal Collections – the half-million pieces of art and treasure acquired by monarchs over the past five centuries, including royal portraits by Holbein and Van Dyck, paintings by Rembrandt, Rubens and Canaletto, and drawings by Leonardo, Raphael and Michelangelo.

The first floor of the gallery has lovely views over the extent of the palace gardens.

Buckingham Palace; tel: 0303 123 7300; www.royalcollection.org.uk. The Queen's Gallery: tel: 0303 123 7301; www.royalcollection.org.uk; daily 10am–5.30pm; map C3

Visit Wellington Barracks, home of the regiments who protect the Queen, and try on a bearskin hat

The tourists line up, sometimes ten-deep, outside the gates of Buckingham Palace to watch the changing of the guard at 11am. The Guard Mounting, as it is more properly called, actually starts at 11.30am and is quite a spectacle. But it can be an uncomfortable scrum from which you cannot always get a good view. Much more sensible then to visit the guards at home in **Wellington Barracks**. If you time your visit for 10.50am (daily Apr–Aug) you will be able to see the Guards getting into formation in preparation for their march up to St James's Palace and Buckingham Palace for the changing of the Guard. Then if your interest in 'the bearskin boys' has been piqued, you could have a look around the **Guards Museum**. Inside, you will learn about the five regiments – the Grenadier Guards, Coldstream Guards, Scots Guards, Irish Guards and Welsh Guards – which, together with the Household Cavalry, the Life Guards, and the Blues and Royals, make up the Household Division of the Army charged with protecting Queen Elizabeth and Prince Philip. On display are uniforms, helmets, instruments, medals, a tent from the Crimean War and the military tunic worn by a 16-year-old Princess Elizabeth to take the salute at the Trooping of the Colour in 1947. And if you have ever wondered what it was like to wear one of those awkward-looking tall bearskin hats, just ask and you will be permitted to try one on. It might give you renewed respect for the guards when you realise just what a trial it is to remain unsmiling under such a heavy and tickly thing.

Wellington Barracks, Birdcage Walk; tel: 020 7414 32428; www.theguardsmuseum. com; daily 10am–4pm; map D3

Pay your respects to poets and kings in Westminster Abbey and be inspired by Westminster Cathedral

As the venue for most of the country's coronations since 1066, **Westminster Abbey** has been the backdrop to the pageant of British history. This glorious medieval church, parts of which date back to 1055, is still dedicated to the celebration of great events in the British nation. Most of the kings and queens of England are buried here and Poet's Corner has memorials to Chaucer, Shakespeare, Byron, Keats, the Brontës, Dickens – almost all the giants of British letters. The Henry VII Chapel is particularly spectacular. The Abbey also has a long musical tradition, and attend ing Evensong, sung by the Boys' Choir of Westminster School, means you can see Westminster Abbey without having to battle the crowds, as it closes to visitors an hour before Evensong begins. (Evensong is every day except Wednesday and Sunday; try to get there by 2.45pm.) There is also a free 30-minute organ recital each Sunday at 5.45pm.

A 15-minute walk away is the less visited **Westminster Cathedral**. The British poet laureate, Sir John Betjeman, best known for his poems celebrating suburban life, was a devoted fan of this early Byzantine-styled Catholic

cathedral. He called it a series of surprises and remarked that 'the greatest surprise of all [is] that the Cathedral looks larger inside than it looks from the outside'. Like the Abbey, Westminster Cathedral has a strong reputation for music. The Sung High Mass is an uplifting experience with incense and legions of altar servers. Most people visit Westminster Cathedral to shimmy up to the top of the bell tower – an excellent vantage point.

Westminster Abbey; tel: 020 7222 5152; www.westminster-abbey.org; map F3 Westminster Cathedral, 42 Francis St; tel: 020 7798 9055; www.westminster cathedral.org.uk; map D2

77

BLOOMSBURY, HOLBORN AND KING'S CROSS

E   **F**   **G**   **H**

5

4

3

2

1

Gray's Inn Road
Swinton Lane
Argyle Street
Acton Street
Cromer Street
King's Cross Road
Harrison Street
Holy Cross
Sidmouth Street

Heathcote St
PANCRAS   CLERKENWELL

ST GEORGE'S GARDENS
Mecklenburgh
Founding Museum
Doughty St
Gray's Inn Road
Wren St
Calthorpe Street
Phoenix Place
Mount Pleasant Post Sorting Office
Farringdon Road
Brunswick Sq.
CORAM'S FIELDS
Rosebery Ave
Warner
Vine St

Charles Dickens Museum
Brownlow Mews
Doughty M
Roger
North M
Clerkenwell Road
Wall
Cross
Hatton
wick tre
Gt Ormond St Hospital for Children
The Lamb
Oliver Spencer
Persephone Books
Bea's of Bloomsbury
Hatton St
The National Hospital
Queen Square
Lamb's Conduit St
Rugby St
Northington
Portpool La.
Greville
Baldwins
Brooke's Ct
Leather
Kirby St
Street
eorge the Martyr
Great Ormond
James
Dombey St
New North St
GRAY'S INN GARDENS
Gray's Inn Road
Southampton Row
Theobald's Road
Raymond Bldgs
Gray's Inn
South Square
Cittie of York
Holborn
Holborn Circus
Bloms bury Square
Vernon
Red Lion Square
Procter St
Eagle St
HOLBORN
omsbury Way
Southampton
Richm
Princeton
Catton St
High Holborn
Southamptn Bldgs
CHANCERY LANE
Furnival St
Norwich St
Fetter Lane
Renaissance London Chancery Court Hotel
Sir John Soane's Museum
Gate St
Whetstone Park
Chancery Lane
Cursitor St
Bream's Bldgs
West Harding Street
Dr Johnson's House
s Smith orn
HOLBORN
Remnant St
Fleet River Bakery
LINCOLN'S INN FIELDS
Lincoln's Inn Hall
New Square
Fleet Street
Kingsway
Portsmouth
mason's all
Lincoln's
Old Curiosity Shop
Portugal Street
Carey St
Lincoln's Inn
St Dunstan-in-the-West
Prince Henry's Room
Bouverie St
Tudor St
Aldwych
Clements Inn
Royal Courts of Justice
Strand
Inn. Temple Hall
Bush House
St Clement Danes
Essex St
Arundel St
Mid. Temple Hall
Middle Temple Lane
Temple Ave
Inner Temple
TEMPLE GARDENS

oomsbury, lborn and Fitzrovia

100   200   300   400   500 yds

100   200   300   400   500 m

Swissôtel The Howard
Somerset House
Temple Place
Middle Temple
Victoria Embankment
Blackfriars
HOS Wellington

E   **F**   TEMPLE   **G**   **H**

Discover sad realities and beautiful art at the Foundling Museum

To walk around the graceful rooms of this fine Georgian building is to risk being overwhelmed by sadness along with fascination. Britain's first **Foundling Hospital** opened on this site in 1741 with a mission to take in abandoned or illegitimate children. When a woman left her baby here she would place a 'foundling token' with it so that, should she ever be able to come back and claim her child, they could match her to it. The tokens were carefully recorded by the hospital. Sadly most of them stayed in the hospital, and they must number among the most poignant museum artefacts it's possible to see. They might be a coin, a button, a ribbon, or a poem; as you look at them you can almost feel the desperation that led these often shabby little objects to be in the care of the hospital.

The Foundling Hospital was founded by Thomas Coram, a sea captain and philanthropist, with support from his two friends William Hogarth and George Friedrich Handel. Hogarth donated a fine portrait of Coram, and some etchings, to the hospital and encouraged his artist friends to donate works too. Thus it became Britain's first ever public art gallery with a nationally important collection that includes a Gainsborough and Joshua Reynolds. The Gerald Coke Handel Collection, bequeathed to the museum in 1996, is a special collection devoted to the great composer, and includes his will and a copy of the score for the Messiah. It has some comfortable 'musical armchairs' – press a button and you can hear the music he wrote for the hospital – a beautiful way to end your visit.

Just opposite there's a playground, **Coram's Fields**, with fountains and a small petting zoo open to any child. Adults can only enter if they are accompanied by a child.

Foundling Museum, 40 Brunswick Square; tel: 020 7841 3600; www.foundlingmuseum. org.uk; Tue–Sat 10am–5pm, Sun from 11am; children under 16 free; map E4

Sample fine British beer and food in a Victorian public house

The diminutive **Newman Arms** is loved for its Victorian décor, and even more so for 20 years for its homemade pies. But when its chefs upped sticks and moved to north London, there was a huge hungry hole that needed to be filled. Up popped Matt Chatfield, from Cornwall, who set up The Cornwall Project to promote, and transport, freshly caught fish from the south-west coast. Now the pub serves fresh seafood, caught that morning, like mackerel with fresh almonds and turbot with olive sauce.

Charles Dickens is said to have imbibed in **The Lamb**, a pub that is Victorian in appearance although thought to be much older. It has many associations with the Blooms-bury set, the literary elite of the mid 20th century. Step inside for a good

pint of ale and upscale British pub food from local ingredients: Billings-gate fish pie or Suffolk honey-glazed gammon with triple-cooked chips.

The high-ceilinged **Cittie of York** with its long, dark wood bar dates back to 1430 although what you see now was built in the 1920s, and Grade-II listed. The Victorian-style snugs – cosy booths seating 6 to 8 people – are a real plus but of course these are the first spots to get taken in this very popular after-work pub. It also has a cellar bar and a ground-floor dining room.

The Newman Arms, 23 Rathbone St; tel:
020 7636 1127; map C2
The Lamb, 94 Lamb's Conduit St; tel: 020
7405 0713; map F4
Cittie of York, 22 High Holborn; tel: 020
7242 7670; map G3

Enjoy a regenerated King's Cross with a dazzling station and new food outlets

When the Eurostar terminal shifted from Waterloo to St Pancras International Station, it didn't just mean a different place to board your under-channel journey to Paris – it was the forefront of a major regeneration project in the King's Cross area. Gone are the days of unsavoury characters loitering around the old station, where you'd beat a hasty retreat after disembarking from your train. The area now boasts elegant paved walkways, light installations, lush restaurants and gloriously refurbished hotels; there's also a renovated warehouse nestling on Regent's Canal, now housing industrial chic restaurants and a prestigious art college.

St Pancras International station is a destination in its own right, with the famous **Searcys Champagne Bar** (1st floor St Pancras Station; tel: 020 7870 9900; pictured) that runs alongside the international platform below the enormous Victorian vaulted roof. There's a slick shopping arcade with outlets of Fortnum & Mason, Hamleys and John Lewis, among other prestigious names.

A quick walk up the pedestrianised King's Boulevard takes you over Regent's Canal to Granary Square, refurbished and adorned with 1,000 choreographed dancing fountains. In summer it hosts outdoor concerts and a floating cinema. The great hulking 1852 Granary Building has been smartly refurbished and now houses a department of Central St Martin's art college, but it is the eating and drinking venues that are the main draw here. Highly recommended is **Caravan** (1 Granary Sq; tel: 020 7101 7661), a popular restaurant and coffee roastery with open brickwork and industrial chic exposed pipes. The menu is all about small sharing plates – go for the soba noodle salad and grilled octopus with chorizo, or a mug of fresh coffee while sitting on a bar stool leaning on sacks of coffee beans. Next door is **The Grain Store** (tel: 020 7324 4466), where chef Bruno Loubet pays homage to the humble vegetable – except dishes are far from dull. Dishes, inspired by his world travels, include fresh fig with smoke aubergine, and carpaccio with fermented beetroot dressing and spiced *labneh*. Just off the square is **Dishoom Godown** (5 Stable St; tel: 020 7420 9321), in an old transit shed, with dishes conjuring old Bombay like *nalli nihari* (lamb on the bone stew with sesame onion seed naan), and okra fries.

From here you're also close to **King's Place**, the entertainment hub with two galleries, intimate music venues and a varied programme of live events, plus a large bar with a terrace overlooking the canal.

Back towards the station are two refurbished hotels with a wonderful array of eateries. The ornate Gothic Revival-style **St Pancras Renaissance Hotel** (www.stpancras london.com) on Euston Rd is a joy to see – take time to admire the exterior before heading to for dinner at the **Gilbert Scott** (tel: 020 7278 3888), named after the original architect, or drinks in the **Booking Office Bar** (tel: 020 7841 3566), once part of the station. Opposite lies the boutique **Great Northern Hotel** (Pancras Rd; tel: 020 3388 0818), where **Plum & Spilt Milk** (tel: 020 3388 0818) serves contemporary British cuisine.

Feel the massed power of 14 million books in the reading rooms of the British Library

There was a great deal of tutting among literary types when the **British Library** left its beautiful setting in the British Museum for a custom-built site near King's Cross. But even the most die-hard critics of the plain red-brick exterior cannot fail to be charmed by the bright accommodating interior. There are five floors beneath the ground and nine above, and the corridors and open spaces are all dotted with chairs complete with bookrest, lamp and plug to charge your laptop. These are not only convenient for study but also for some of the best people-watching in the city. Academics, writers and book-lovers from all over the world come here and they make interesting viewing (anyone can visit the building, but to use the reading rooms you need to apply for a Reader's Pass; see the website for details).

The not-so-studious can linger at the forecourt's **Last Word Café** with views of Eduardo Paolozzi's imposing bronze of Isaac Newton, beautiful in summer, or at the first-floor's **King's Library** restaurant – it's next to the six-level glass tower containing many thousands of precious books belonging to King George III. Entry to that, unfortunately, is strictly controlled.

At any one time there are several exhibitions, comprising permanent collections and temporary exhibitions. A real highlight is the **Treasures of the British Library** collection (housed in the **Sir John Ritblat library**), which holds precious tomes from the Magna Carta, Leonardo da Vinci's notebooks, and Shakespeare's first folio. Back to the modern era, there's also a crumpled piece of paper on which Paul McCartney scrawled the first lyrics to *Help*.

The ground floor shop has excellent books and gifts relating to their temporary exhibitions. There are also regular guided tours of the public areas.

British Library, 96 Euston Rd; tel: 020 7412 7454; www.bl.uk; Mon–Fri 9.30am–6pm, to 8pm Tue, Sun 11am–5pm; map D5

Get to know Sir John Soane, an obsessive art collector, and his myriad curious artefacts

Going to **Sir John Soane's Museum** is a pretty eccentric, very British experience. It is a narrow space so crammed with precious things that unless you go early you might be asked to wait in a queue (when full, they operate a one in/one out policy). Before you enter, a smartly dressed usher will politely and firmly tell you to take off all hanging bags and put them in a carrier bag to decrease the risk of you accidentally knocking anything over. And if you ask a member of staff where the Canaletto paintings are, they might inform you to locate the statue of Apollo, lower your gaze, and, 'the landscapes are to the left of his bottom'.

Sir John Soane was an architect, most notably of the Bank of England, but he is best known for his hobby – collecting art and antiquities around the world. Soane collected so many during his lifetime (1753–1837) that his house was known as the 'academy of Architecture'. One of his proudest acquisitions was an ala-baster sarcophagus found in Egypt's Valley of the Kings. The British Mu-seum decided not to buy it, allowing Soane to snatch it up, a purchase that so elated him he threw a party that lasted three days. That's the kind of guy he was, and to visit this jewel-box of a house-museum is to take a trip into one man's obses-sions. On the first Tuesday of every month, the museum is open until 9pm and lit by candles, making it an even more spookily atmospheric place to admire a gargoyle, a mum-mified cat or an ancient treasure in hushed tones.

Nearby is one of London's nicest independent coffee bars, the tiny **Fleet River Bakery**, where all the food – cakes, bread, soup, frittatas and salads – is freshly baked or made from scratch on the premises every day.

Sir John Soane's Museum, 13 Lincoln's Inn Fields; tel: 020 7405 2107; www.soane.org; Tue–Sat 10am–5pm; free; map F2
Fleet River Bakery, 71 Lincoln's Inn Fields; map F2

Take a tour of the greatest civilisations of the world at the British Museum

The Great Court at the **British Museum** is the largest enclosed courtyard in Europe, and, with its magnificent glass roof, is a fittingly grand entrance to one of the greatest displays of antiquities in the world. There are eight million objects here that between them document the rise and fall of all the greatest civilisations. 'Only' about 80,000 of them are on display, but to do it all justice and have even the quickest squint at every one would take years. Here follows a suggested tour covering all areas which can be done in half a day:

Start in **Ancient Civilisations** on the ground floor, reached via the Great Court. Room 4 has the Egyptian sculptures including a magnificent bust of Rameses II, and the Rosetta Stone, which was discovered by Napoleon's army in the Nile Delta and provided the key to deciphering Egyptian hieroglyphs. Next up are the Greeks in Gallery 18 and the Elgin Marbles – an exquisitely detailed frieze from the colonnade of the Parthenon. In 2015 there was an unsuccessful bid by the Greek government to reclaim them.

Go up the West Stairs and into the **Ancient Near East** rooms where you can see beautiful Turkish and North African mosaics on your way through to the **Egyptian Galleries** (62 and 63) where the mummies lie resplendent and you can learn all about how it was done thanks to an at-a-glance guide on the wall. Further on is gallery 56 and the exquisite *Babylonian Queen of the Night*, a generously curved woman on a clay plaque. Walk back through galleries 63 and 66 to reach the North Stairs which are dominated by the giant Chinese figure of the Amitabha Buddha.

In Room 40 tacticians and gameplayers should stop to admire the 11th-century Lewis Chessmen.

Descend to the **Hotung Gallery** (33) to see a gracefully expressive gilt-and-bronze statue of the Buddhist goddess Tara from Sri Lanka. Exit the Hotung gallery and walk downstairs into the **Wellcome Trust Gallery** (24) to see the sacred if rather grumpy aspect of the Easter Island Statue. And don't miss the Mexican sculpture of Tlazolteotl in Room 27 before returning to the Great Court for a coffee and sandwich.

You shouldn't leave, however, without a quick look round the **Enlightenment Gallery**. It celebrates the great age of discovery when British naturalists, historians and scholars scoured the world for objects to help them to better understand life as it is, and was, lived. There is a replica of the Rosetta Stone that you are allowed to touch, and a hands-on table where you can have a feel of fossils, coins, arrowheads, tiles or pots. Its temporary exhibitions are popular, and advance online booking is recommended.

British Museum, Great Russell St; tel: 020 7328 8181; www.britishmuseum.org; daily 10am–5.30pm; most galleries open Fri until 8.30pm; map D3

Take a walk in the hidden tranquillity of the Inns of Court

If you were accidentally beamed into the **Inns of Court** and told to guess where you were, you'd think you had landed in the quads of an ancient university. But this hidden enclave is where London barristers train and practise. There are four Inns – **Lincoln's Inn**, **Gray's Inn**, **Inner Temple** and **Middle Temple** – each with quiet gardens, medieval chapels and Tudor libraries and halls. And, despite some rather stern signs (one forbids the entrance of 'rude children'), you are welcome to pace the paths and picnic on the grass on weekdays (each Inn has slightly different entrance times, so check websites).

The halls are off bounds, unless you book a tour (London Walks; tel: 020 7624 3978) but the chapels are open to the public.

All the Inns of Court are steeped in history. The Jacobean poet, John Donne, was pastor of the Gothic Chapel at Lincoln's Inn, and his famous lines 'Never send to know for whom the bell tolls; it tolls for thee' were inspired by the bells that were rung to alert barristers of the death of one of their own. In 1601 Shakespeare oversaw the royal premiere of *Twelfth Night* at Middle Temple Hall where Queen Elizabeth I was a frequent guest. Dickens's first job was as a clerk in Gray's Inn, and he used the Tudor Hall in Lincoln's Inn as the setting for *Bleak House*. But whether you are interested in olden times or just want to rest a while in a peaceful garden – the Inns of Court are one of the city's most rewarding hidden treasures.

Inner Temple; tel: 020 7797 8250; www.innertemple.org.uk; map G1
Middle Temple; tel: 020 7427 4800; www.middletemple.org.uk; map G1
Lincoln's Inn; tel: 020 7405 1393; www.lincolnsinn.org.uk; map G2
Gray's Inn; tel: 020 7458 7800; www.graysinn.info; map G2

Savour the delights of a quirkily charming thoroughfare, Lamb's Conduit Street

Lamb's Conduit Street (LCS) is an enclave of independent shops – the vast majority are pure London originals. If variety is the spice of life, this street has a little bit of everything you fancy.

There has been a recent trend for men's clothing on LCS and guys could completely get themselves kitted out. **Oliver Spencer** (62) is mostly menswear of a cool, relaxed, military inspired kind, while **Folk** (49) sells affordable 'unrestrictive' modern leisure wear. Folk Clothing has men's (49) and women's (53) upscale fashionable clothing including casual suits and attractive panel dresses – and there's also a men's barber. There are two bespoke tailors for suits made to suit you, sir: **Connock & Lockie** (84a) was established in 1902 and creates suiting from the very first stage of pattern making; and **Sims & MacDonald** (46) specialises in luxury fabrics, cashmere and wool and camelhair for coats. **Simon Cart** (36a) has everything for the well-dressed man about town, from lambswool jumpers to a textured bobble tie clip.

Feed your mind at **Persephone Books** (59), a publishing house and bookseller with a mission to reprint neglected women writers such as Monica Dickens and Noel Streatfeild in beautifully designed editions.

For many, **The Lamb** is the main attraction on LCS, a lovely old pub of the kind that are disappearing too fast and becoming relics of the past. There are other options for food and drink: **Cigala** (54) is a Spanish restaurant with intriguing tapas and Spanish cocktails. **Tutti's** (68), pictured, is a homely bustling café for pasta, coffee and paninis – good for a pit stop. For something more substantial, relax your weary legs (and rest your shopping bags) at **La Gourmandina** (57) for a lunchtime baguette, a selection of artisan Italian cured meats and – for those with a real appetite – rabbit stuffed with Tuscan sausage.

Tap into London's literary treasure at the Charles Dickens Museum

Dickens was an energetic and restless soul. Before becoming the novelist and showman he is best known as, he had several jobs, and followed many interests – philanthropic, theatrical and academic – to which he devoted much time and on which he wrote copious essays. He had ten children, one wife and several intense friendships with women about which there was much speculation. He moved his family into 48 Doughty Street in 1837. And though he only lived in it for two years, he managed in that time to complete *The Pickwick Papers*, write the whole of *Oliver Twist*

and *Nicholas Nickleby*, commence *Barnaby Rudge*, and father three children. This was a prodigious output by any standards, and you can detect some of the great man's intense energy as you admire the little desk beneath the window overlooking the back garden where he sat and wrote every day. Throughout December the **Charles Dickens Museum** holds special events, decorating the house with special Victorian furnishings. A huge attraction is the reading of *A Christmas Carol* to raise money for charity; this sells out quickly. There are also atmospheric candlelit evening openings.

Fans of the Victorian age in need of a pick-me-up should make a beeline for **Bea's of Bloomsbury**, a pretty little tearoom where they can enjoy good old-fashioned tea and cake: mini meringues, Valrhona brownies and delicate sandwiches. There's an open-air pastry kitchen and an informal café setting.

Charles Dickens Museum, 48 Doughty Street; tel: 020 7405 2127; www.dickens museum.com; daily 10am–5pm; map F4 Bea's of Bloomsbury, 44 Theobald's Road; tel: 020 7242 8330; map F3

Gain a little more understanding of the definition of London life at Dr Johnson's House

Dr Johnson must be one of the most quoted men in the English language – his immortal line, "When a man is tired of London, he is tired of life" is trotted out by all those who love the capital. It was in the garret of this charming early 18th-century town house that Dr Johnson laboured for nine years to produce the world's first comprehensive dictionary of the English language. Reproductions of the first edition with its 42,773 definitions lie open on the table in the study so you can choose your own favourite words. One phrase not in there is Tourette Syndrome, although Johnson with his frequent tics and involuntary gestures has been posthumously diagnosed with the condition. This is thought to be the reason he was unable to follow his chosen profession of teacher and was forced to become a writer, a job in which he could remain largely out of view, and unteased by children.

There is plenty of life in this house. Sadly Dr Johnson's beloved wife Elizabeth, or Tetty, died in 1752. Overcome with grief, his response was to fill his home with people. He took in random relatives and lodgers and surrounded himself with company. There

are well-written and interesting explanatory cards in each room describing who lived there and the parties and activities that took place. It is a fascinating insight into a lost world – especially if you take some quiet time in the library and soak up the tranquillity. If you want to take it outdoors, there is a walk around all Dr Johnson's favourite places – pubs and printing houses mostly – at 3pm on the first Wednesday of every month.

Dr Johnson's House, 17 Gough Square; tel: 020 7353 3745; www.drjohnsonshouse. org; Mon–Sat 11am–5.30pm, Oct–Apr until 5pm; map G2

Discover one-of-a-kind shops in historic buildings

This is just a guess, but it's possible you might need an umbrella while in London. If you forgot to pack one or fancy buying a special new one, proceed directly to **James Smith & Sons** (53 New Oxford St; map E2), which has been in business since 1830. The shop is packed to the gunwales with umbrellas of all shapes, sizes and colours. Some of them are still made on the premises, and you can watch as one of the staff stitches the handmade items together. They cost up to around £250, so if you do buy one, try not to leave it on the tube the next day.

You are unlikely to actually need a toy, but they are always nice to look at. Especially at **Pollock's Toy Museum and Toy Shop** (1 Scala St; map C3), which takes up two four-storey 18th-century houses and is most famous for its collection of Victorian model theatres. Children love looking at the weird and wonderful playthings of the past, and there's a shop next door selling modern replicas.

The area around British Museum has many antiquarian bookshops, reflecting its strong literary heritage. Sadly many of these are closing, due to high rents and less custom. But one place to have stood the test of time is **Jarndyce** (46 Great Russell St; map D2), antiquarian booksellers established in 1969. The building dates back to 1730 and it's been a bookshop since 1890; the 19th-century illustrator Randolph lived and worked here – you'll see the blue plaque outside. Look out also for the ghost of a Scotsman in a kilt – it's said to be haunted.

Uncover tucked-away museums and medical marvels

If you're a fan of ancient Egypt but find the crowds at the British Museum too much, then there is a gem of a collection in the University College London. Tucked away in the UCL's campus is the **Petrie Museum of Egyptian Archaeology**, which crams around 80,000 objects into its display cases. This is about as far removed from a high-tech, multimedia interactive museum as you can get, but that is its charm. The emphasis is on the pieces – after all this is one of the world's greatest collections of Egyptian and Sudanese archaeology. It has the world's oldest wills, on papyrus, and a headnet dress of a dancer from 2400 BC, as well as the world's largest collection of Roman period mummy portraits.

The university also houses the **Grant Museum of Zoology** – a veritable feast for anyone who likes to gaze at strange 'dead things' in ball jars. It was founded in 1828 as a teaching collection, and now the museum is filled with skeletons, mounted animals and specimens preserved in fluid.

Close by, the **Wellcome Collection** houses the personal collection of Dr Henry Wellcome – an eye-watering historical display of medical implements from around the world. While asking yourself, "Did they really use one of those?" and flinching at the tools used for assisting childbirth and amputations (saws and stirrups), it does make you appreciate medical research and progress. It also holds evening events and temporary exhibitions, plus an outstanding bookshop and huge café.

Petrie Museum of Egyptian Archaeology, UCL, Malet Place; tel: 020 7679 2884; www.ucl.ac.uk; Tues–Sat 1–5pm; map C4
Grant Museum of Zoology, UCL, Malet Place; tel: 020 3108 2052; Mon–Sat 1–5pm; map C4
Wellcome Collection, 183 Euston Rd; tel: 020 7611 2222; http://wellcomecollection.org; Tues–Sat 10am–6pm, Thur until 10pm, Sun 11am–6pm; map C4

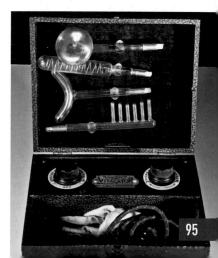

THE CITY, CLERKENWELL AND SPITALFIELDS

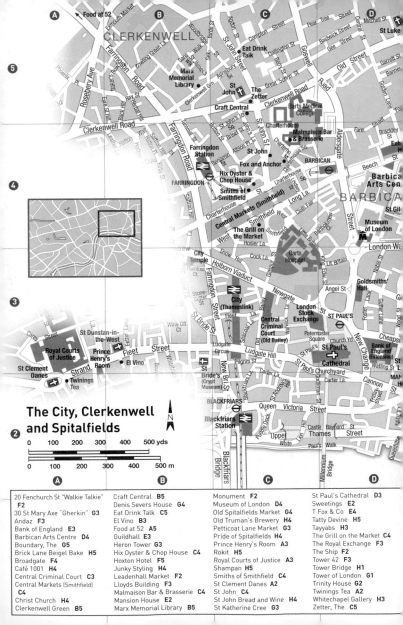

The City, Clerkenwell and Spitalfields

0 100 200 300 400 500 yds

0 100 200 300 400 500 m

20 Fenchurch St "Walkie Talkie" F2	Craft Central B5	Monument F2	St Paul's Cathedral D3
30 St Mary Axe "Gherkin" G3	Denis Severs House G4	Museum of London D4	Sweetings E2
Andaz F3	Eat Drink Talk C5	Old Spitalfields Market G4	T Fox & Co E4
Bank of England E3	El Vino B3	Old Truman's Brewery H4	Tatty Devine H5
Barbican Arts Centre D4	Food at 52 A5	Petticoat Lane Market G3	Tayyabs H3
Boundary, The G5	Guildhall E3	Pride of Spitalfields H4	The Grill on the Market C4
Brick Lane Beigel Bake H5	Heron Tower G3	Prince Henry's Room A3	The Royal Exchange F3
Broadgate F4	Hix Oyster & Chop House C4	Rokit H5	The Ship F2
Café 1001 H4	Hoxton Hotel F5	Royal Courts of Justice A3	Tower 42 F3
Central Criminal Court C3	Junky Styling H4	Shampan H5	Tower Bridge H1
Central Markets (Smithfield) C4	Leadenhall Market F2	Smiths of Smithfield C4	Tower of London G1
Christ Church H4	Lloyds Building F3	St Clement Danes A2	Trinity House G2
Clerkenwell Green B5	Malmaison Bar & Brasserie C4	St John C4	Twinings Tea A2
	Mansion House E2	St John Bread and Wine H4	Whitechapel Gallery H3
	Marx Memorial Library B5	St Katherine Cree G3	Zetter, The C5

Find religion, revolution and jewels in Clerkenwell Green

Clerkenwell Green is a discreet, almost hidden square (which isn't actually green at all) that incongruously combines ancient knights, foreign revolutionaries and trendy craftspeople. It has been continuously inhabited for centuries. On the northern edge of the green you can still see remnants of the medieval well from which Clerkenwell gets its name, and relics of the 11th-century St John's church and hospital, just off it on St John's Lane. The 16th-century **Priory of the Knights of St John of Jerusalem** that was built to replace that church still stands, and there is a small museum devoted to the history of the Order of St John and the Knights Templars who would gather on Clerkenwell Green before setting off on their crusades. The oldest building currently standing on Clerkenwell Green was built in 1737 as a charity school and now houses the **Marx Memorial Library**. Marx's

friend Lenin produced a magazine, *Iskra*, here, and the little room where he laboured has been saved for posterity and is open to the public, as is the library. Tours are held every Tuesday and Thursday at 1pm.

In the 18th century Clerkenwell Green was the centre of the English watchmaking industry, and there are still precision instrument makers and jewellers in the area. **Craft Central** is a not-for-profit association dedicated to preserving the nature of Clerkenwell and providing cheap workspaces for jewellers, silversmiths and watchmakers. They moved their studio to a couple of streets from Clerkenwell Green, but still have regular open days and 'Made in Clerkenwell' exhibitions (check their website for details) across three spaces in Craft Central's two historic Clerkenwell buildings. The Corner Shop has a new pop-up shop every week, and twice a year Made in Clerkenwell showcases works of the design community.

Marx Memorial Library, 37a Clerkenwell Green; tel: 020 7253 1485; www.marx-memorial-library.org; Mon–Thur 1–6pm; free
Craft Central, 33–35 St John's Square; www.craftcentral.org.uk
All map B5

A glittering bar and glimmering shops at The Royal Exchange

During the 17th century, stockbrokers were not allowed in **The Royal Exchange** due to their 'rude manners'. Nowadays it is open to all as, since 2001, it was reinvented as a luxury shopping mall full of bijoux boutiques wrapped around the smart brasserie at its centre. Which is very apt as this grand, Grade I-listed building has always been a temple to London's wealth. In the centre of the soaring atrium is the Grand Café, a gleaming bar and crustacea bar, but the best tables are on the first-floor gallery overlooking the action. The plush shops at The Royal Exchange are mostly devoted to jewels, fashion and fragrance with Tiffany, Smythson, Tateossian

and Bulgari; Jo Malone, Gucci, Hermès, Paul Smith and Lulu Guinness – it's rather like a mini version of Bond Street without traffic or rain to contend with.

If you want to fit yourself out like one of those 'rude' stockbrokers, try Church's which has all the accessories a City gent requires, starting with hand-crafted leather shoes. And to nosh like one, try **Threadneedle Bar**'s (tel: 020 7618 2480) signature cocktails and vintage champagne, along with rock oysters and soft shell crab.

The Royal Exchange (where Cornhill and Threadneedle St meet); www.the royalexchange.co.uk; store: 10am–6pm, restaurants and bars: 8am–11pm; map F3

Restaurant-hop your way around London's last-surviving meat market in Smithfield

In *Oliver Twist*, Dickens described Smithfield Market as being 'ankle deep in filth and mire', but don't let this put you off. **Smithfield** is still a working market, one of London's oldest, where meat has been bought and sold for over 800 years. However, it has managed to put aside its unseemly reputation for blood and filth and become a restaurant-rich playground for the young and hungry.

St John (26 St John St; tel: 020 7251 0848/4998) is perhaps the most famous of Smithfield restaurants. Opened in 1994 in a former Georgian smokehouse, it is presided over by Fergus Henderson, whose 'nose-to-tail eating' has inspired chefs the world over and has spawned a city of offal lovers. Diners lured by the lavish praise heaped on St John (it has one Michelin star) may be surprised at the extreme modesty of the white-walled surrounds as well as the plainness of the food – the focus is on seasonal British ingredients, and they come simply cooked and presented. The roast bone marrow with parsley is the most famous dish and has quite a following, as does the dessert plate of Eccles cake with Lancashire cheese, but you can also find excellent fish and unusual vegetables. **St John Bread and Wine** (94–96 Commercial St; tel: 020 7251 0848; pictured) is a more relaxed, informal outpost where you can pick up a loaf and a bottle on your way to a picnic or stop in for a bacon sandwich or meal.

Smiths of Smithfield (67–77 Charterhouse St; tel: 020 7251 7950) is on four storeys of a Grade II-listed building, each with a different offering. There's a buzzing bar with decent pub food on the ground floor where you cannot book so have to dive on a table as soon as it is vacat-

ed; a brasserie on the second floor; a lounge on the third; and a restaurant with a wraparound terrace on the fourth where the atmosphere is serene and the star is British beef.

British produce is also the focus at **Hix Oyster & Chop House** (35–37 Greenhill's Rents Cowcross St; tel: 020 7017 1930). Overseen by Mark Hix, former chef of the Ivy (see page 58), and author of the highly influential recipe book, *British Regional Food*, it combines no-nonsense dining with occasional flourishes of old-fashioned white-tableclothed and silver-plated British class.

For more a slab of steak than its innards, **The Grill on the Market** (2–3 West Smithfield; tel: 020 7246 0900) is one of a small national chain. It takes pride in its 28-day aged steak, also fresh fish and seafood that's smoked on site. Their 'Best of British' section on the menu has items such as sirloin aged on the bone, wagyu fillet – the 'daddy of all steaks' – and beef burgers with pulled pork topping. Not for the vegetarians among you!

Work out where the next Picasso or Hirst is coming from at the Whitechapel Gallery

The **Whitechapel Gallery** was founded by young clergyman Samuel Barnet in 1901, who saw it as a way of bringing light to the people of East London and lifting them out of their grinding poverty. It has since made its name with an unerring eye for the best of the avant-garde, and for exhibiting emerging artists from around the world. It hosted Picasso's scathing anti-war painting *Guernica* on its world tour in 1939, and in 1956 was the first place to show Pop Art in London. It then went on, over the years, to introduce Jackson Pollock, Mark Rothko, Robert Rauschenberg and Frieda Kahlo to Britain.

Following a £13 million refit, the Whitechapel is now an even more inviting space. At any one time there are several small exhibitions – usually covering a wide range of media – and the ground-floor café bar is a buzzing place to meet (it has free WiFi, so there are usually a few laptops around). The gallery also organises First Thursdays (the first Thursday of each month), where around 150 East London galleries hold free events, exhibitions and talks for a special late opening.

Whitechapel Gallery, 77–82 Whitechapel High St; tel: 020 7552 7888; www.white chapelgallery.org; Tue–Sun 11am–6pm, Thur until 9pm; free; map H3

First Thursdays

Check these East London galleries for First Thursday events: **Space Studio** (129–131 Mare St; 020 8525 4330) for multimedia exhibitions and talks; **Rivington Place** (Rivington Place; 020 7749 1240), the global diversity of art; **Raven Row** (56 Artilley Lane), a non-profit contemporary art space in an 18th-century building; **Waterside Contemporary** (2 Clunbury St; 020 3417 0159) hosts a diverse crow-section of art events.

Climb up to the Whispering Gallery and marvel at the magnificence of St Paul's Cathedral

So much of London was lost in the Great Fire of 1666, a shocking few days of devastation. But perhaps one consolation for modern Londoners was the loss of the original **St Paul's Cathedral** on this site, because it allowed Sir Christopher Wren to come up with its replacement. He originally devised a scheme considered so radical and overreaching that it had to be toned down. Nevertheless, of the 50 churches he built after the Great Fire, St Paul's remains his masterpiece. For many years this was London's tallest building.

Start a visit by going directly to the centre, stand under the dome, and look up, before you head off exploring every nave and cranny. If you plan to climb the dome, do it while you still have the energy. Three hundred steps up a winding staircase later, you emerge into the Whispering Gallery, so called because the faintest whisper can be heard opposite across the huge circle. A further 231 steps up is the golden gallery which rewards you with a panoramic view of London. A free 90-minute guided tour takes you to the Chapel of St Michael and the quire, areas not usually open to the public.

Try and catch a music recital here; there are regular services with the choir (especially around Christmas and Easter), and a free organ recital (Sunday 4.45pm).

St Paul's Cathedral, Ludgate Hill; tel: 020 7246 8357; www.stpauls.co.uk; Mon–Sat 8.30am–4.30pm; map D3

Drink and dine with a view at the top of futuristic skyscrapers

When a slew of new buildings went up in London, all glistening silver shafts, it provoked a wave of discussion about the architecture and also opened the way for new wining and dining venues. After all, everyone loves a view. London welcomed **Heron Tower** (110 Bishopsgate; map G3) in 2011, at 230 metres/756 ft – the tallest building in the financial district. Its dining venues soon followed, with **Duck & Waffle** (tel: 020 3640 7310), open 24/7 on the 40th floor with floor-to-ceiling windows to get a real eyeful of the views. Two floors down is **Sushisamba** (tel: 020 3640 7330) serving an intriguing fusion of Brazilian and Japanese food – although they have a rather snooty dress code (über stylish only).

Drawing a slew of comments – mainly uncomplimentary – regarding its design when it was completed in 2014, the 160-metre-high (525 ft) **"Walkie Talkie"** (20 Fenchurch St; map F2) has concave steel sides; it infamously 'melted' a car when the sun's rays were magnified from it. Don't worry too much about that when you ascend to the spectacular, glass-domed **Sky Garden** (tel: 020 7337 2344; pictured) on its 34th floor with viewing platforms, bars and restaurants.

Completed in 1980, and standing at 183 metres (600 ft) high, **Tower 42** (25 Old Broad St; map F3) – formerly known as NatWest Tower – is a city landmark where you dine at Jason Atherton's **City Social** (tel: 020 7877 7703) on the 24th floor; his modern European dishes are superb. Higher up, sup bubbly at **Vertigo 42** sky-high champagne bar (tel: 020 7877 7842). Booking is essential – ask for the seats nearest the elevator for the best view.

Want more? Check out the dining options at **The Shard** for the mother of all views (see page 120).

Take refreshment in the 11th-century crypt of Sir Christopher Wren's St Mary-Le-Bow

This beautiful little church has the Great Bells of Bow which, according to the popular nursery rhyme *Oranges and Lemons*, say 'I do not know' to the bells of Stepney's question 'Pray when will that be?'. They are also the bells that, if you are born within earshot of them, define you as a cockney or a true Londoner. The Bow Bells crashed to the ground when the church was bombed during the Blitz, but have since been restored on high without any damage to their lovely sound. But there is more to **St Mary-Le-Bow** than bells, for it is also a beautiful place to sit and reflect. Sir Christopher Wren based his design on Rome's Basilica of Maxentius, and apart from the elaborate bell tower it has a restrained elegance unusual in his churches. Another very good reason to visit is **The Café Below**, in the crypt, which has delicious daily dishes, from a breakfast of brioche French toast with bacon, to pan-fried sea bass with clams for dinner. Everything is made from organic local sources.

And if that puts pep in your step, you might want to consider the 311 steps at the nearby **Monument**. Another creation of Sir Christopher Wren, he built this in the 1670s to commemorate the loss of buildings and life caused by the Great Fire. A climb up this beautiful, simple Doric pillar richly rewards you with a breathtaking view illustrating just how the city has regenerated itself since the days of London's Burning. Oh, and you get a certificate for your troubles.

St Mary-Le-Bow, Cheapside; tel: 020 7248 5139; www.stmarylebow.co.uk
The Place Below; tel: 020 7329 0789; www.cafebelow.co.uk; 7.30am–9pm; map D3
The Monument, Fish Street Hill; www.themonument.info; daily 9.30am–5.30pm; map F2

Catch a concert, film, exhibition or play at the Barbican Centre

The running joke about the **Barbican Centre** has been that as big as it is – and it is the largest arts centre in Europe – you could never find it. The vast concrete complex was built on a gaping site that had been bombed in World War II. Despite numerous design problems, it is still Britain's finest example of Brutalist concrete architecture, unrivalled for its scale. At the heart of a residential complex comprising 2,000 flats, the Barbican arts centre is a cultural cornucopia, including two art galleries, two theatres for contemporary drama and dance, cinema showing arthouse films, library and the London Symphony Orchestra. Its music programme is one of the highlights, with interesting series of musicians in unusual genres. There are often free foyer gigs also.

There is a wide range of venues for wining and dining, including a **Martini bar**, Italian 'bistronomy' restaurant **Osteria**, and **Bonfire**, for burgers and shakes. The lakeside terrace is a great place to take your drink, among the fountains, waterbirds and greenery.

The Barbican Centre, Silk Street; tel: 020 7638 8891; www.barbican.org.uk; map D4

Be dazzled by historical bling at the Tower of London

When William the Conqueror began building his white stone tower in the middle of his London fortress in the 1070s, he wanted it not only to dominate the London skyline, but also the hearts and minds of his subjects. Even ruthless, ambitious William would be amazed at how successful he has been in this. Nearly a thousand years later the **White Tower** still stands proud and is one of London's World Heritage Sites. The tower has been seriously overshadowed by towers of a completely different kind all around it, but it continues to speak eloquently of Britain's history to the two million people a year who walk its halls.

The Armoury Room showing the knights and horses in their shining suits of armour is really awe-inspiring, as is St John's Chapel – one of the best-preserved Anglo-Norman churches in Britain. However, most people come to the Tower of London to gawp at **The Crown Jewels** – all the tiaras, crowns, orbs and sceptres owned and sported by British royalty for the past 700 years are twinkling away on display here. Crowd speed is 'controlled' by a slow-moving walkway that edges you past without anyone blocking the view. Another treat is the view over the ramparts to the River Thames from the East Wall walk. Watch out for the Royal Ravens; legend has it that, if they ever leave, the tower will crumble. You can also book ahead for the nightly Ceremony of the Keys (check website for details).

For refreshment, seek out the **New Armouries Café**, near Lanthorne tower, with ingredients sourced from London's food markets.

Tower of London, Tower Hill; tel: 020 3166 6000; www.hrp.org.uk/TowerOfLondon; Tue–Sat 9am–5.30pm, Sun–Mon 10am–5.30pm; charge; map G1

Dig deep into the city's archaeological layers at the Museum of London

London is not just a big city with a long history, it is an intensely complicated and multi-layered place; it comprises peoples from all over the world living in villages joined together into a huge metropolis, and affected in varying ways by centuries of history. Nowhere is this more apparent than in the basement galleries of the **Museum of London**, which aim to tell the tumultuous, dramatic story of London and its people from 1665 to the present day. It is a story of constantly being knocked down and picking itself up again; of destruction and reinvention such as that brought about by the plague, or the Great Fire or the Blitz.

A 240-year-old printing press spills news stories across the gallery ceiling in a clever collision of new and old technologies. And all the while you are walking over glass cases holding the city's archaeology underfoot. There is all the glamour of the theatre (lots of lavish costumes) and commerce (an amazing Art Deco lift that once raised shoppers in Selfridges) but this is counterbalanced by a room filled with the voices of London's dispossessed so you can also take in the meaning of a life of poverty in the shadows of one of the richest cities in the world. To take you really up to the minute, there is an innovative multimedia piece, LDN24, screened on a 160ft elliptical LED screen that explores a 24-hour cycle of London life with 35 live feeds following the pulse of the city. There's also an interactive installation comprised of a constantly changing collage of hundreds of photographs submitted by Londoners.

Museum of London, London Wall; tel: 020 7001 9844; www.museumoflondon.org.uk; daily 10am–6pm, free; map D4

Bag anything from a piece of contemporary art to chic vintage clothing to a tasty pie at Spitalfields

The shops inside **Spitalfields Market** are open all week, and now stalls are there daily also, with a huge variety of cutting-edge fashion, original artwork, homeware and food. Still regarded as a showcase for up-and-coming young artists from the nearby art and design college, the market has lots of vintage, retro and modern original clothes. It is also very strong on jewellery and has stalls selling every style of human adornment you can imagine. It gets busy for its Saturday Style Market, with around 90 independent designers. Look out for the Arts Market, held Thur–Sun twice a month. Whenever you come, Spitalfields is chock-full of good things to eat and global flavours. Some are open daily and some are

'pop ups' – try reliable chains such as **Carluccio's** and **Itsu**, or independent eateries like **Hao Chii** for fusion Asian, and the **Duck Truck** for roast duck wraps and Scotch eggs (duck eggs, of course).

Opposite the market is **Christ Church Spitalfields** by Nicholas Hawksmoor, Sir Christopher Wren's most talented pupil, second only to him as architect of the city's finest churches. Its restored crypt is now open to the public, and there are regular tours.

Spitalfields, 65 Brushfield Street; tel: 020 7377 1496; www.spitalfields.co.uk
Christ Church Spitalfields, Commercial St; www.ccspitalfields.org; map G4

The East End's Sunday markets

Brick Lane: hundreds of stallholders selling a glorious muddle of bric-a-brac and desirable objets d'arts. Map H3–H5
Up Market: indoor market at the Old Truman Brewery with vintage galore, music and crafts. Map H4
Petticoat Lane: Middlesex Street; cheap clothes and accessories and Asian fabrics. Map G3
Columbia Road: flowers, plants and all gardeners' delights plus cool cafés and boutique shops. Map page 152, F4

Time travel to the 18th and 19th centuries in the remarkable Dennis Severs House

London is full of historic house museums dedicated to their former owners – the Dickens, Handel, Sir John Soane museums – which recreate a moment in time and tell a story. But none of them transports you back the way **Dennis Severs House** does. The minute you walk into this remarkable house, inhabited by wealthy Huguenot silk weavers from 1724 until 1919 (by which time the silk trade was dying and they were no longer wealthy), your senses are bombarded – cold, dark, unfamiliar smells and faintly spooky sounds – and you are immersed in a real physical sense of the past. Severs, who died in 1991, wanted people to walk around his house in silence so that they could fully absorb the atmosphere, and there are still signs hand-painted by him with his motto, 'You either see it or you don't', in each of the 11 rooms on four storeys. These take you through the five generations of one family, the fictional Jervises, and from the Enlightenment with its strong bright colour schemes on the ground floor to the outbreak of World War I in the attic rooms. A truly remarkable experience (evening and daytime tours; booking required).

Dennis Severs House, 18 Folgate St; tel: 020 7247 4013; www.dennissevershouse. co.uk; map G4

Shop by day and bar-hop by night in Brick Lane

It's no wonder that Monica Ali chose this run-down cobbled East London street as lead character for her 2003 award-winning novel, *Brick Lane*. It tells quite a story, with its mix of elegant houses built by the Huguenots, synagogues, and sari shops: a tale of successive waves of immigrants and changing fortunes. For most of the last century the only reasons to come here were the large chaotic Sunday Upmarket (vintage clothing and food stalls in the Truman Brewery) or a cheap curry. But since the 1990s, galleries, boutiques, cafés and clubs have been springing up. You're never short of things to do – whether you've come to hunt for vintage treasure (see box) or make a night of it.

If you're seeking a snack either side of midnight, try the 24-hour **Brick Lane Beigel Bake** (159) for warm, filled bagels – salt beef is popular. **Café 1001** (91) dishes up breakfast, coffees and beats to E1's starving artists. Tucked away off Brick Lane, **Pride of Spitalfields** (3 Heneage St) is a friendly, cosy old-world pub. Dotted along Brick Lane is an increasing number of bijou bars with bottled beer, happy-hour cocktails and fruity sheesha pipes.

The southern end of Brick Lane is still very much 'Banglatown', with wall-to-wall curry houses and men trying to beguile you into one. One worth a try is **Shampan** (79) for fantastic Bangladeshi fish curries. There's also the legendary **Tayyabs** (83 Fieldgate St; tel: 020 7247 9543) with its cheap but wonderful smoky grilled meats, dhals and naan breads.

Brick Lane; map H3–H5

Vintage boutiques

Dedicated followers of fashion should check out the following: **Tatty Devine** (236 Brick Lane) for gorgeous cheeky costume jewels; **Junky Styling** (The Old Truman Brewery, 91 Brick Lane) for customised vintage; **The Laden Showroom** (103 Brick Lane) for young designers at the cutting edge; **Rokit** (101 & 107 Brick Lane), possibly London's biggest collection of vintage; **Beyond Retro** (Cheshire St, off Brick Lane) – two open-plan rooms in a former dairy with eclectic vintage fashion.

BANKSIDE, SOUTH BANK AND WATERLOO

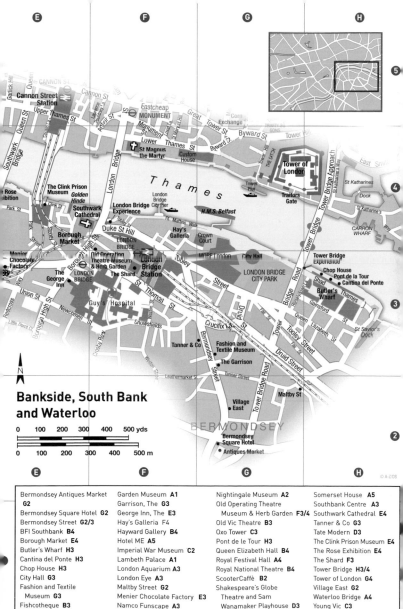

Bankside, South Bank and Waterloo

0 100 200 300 400 500 yds

0 100 200 300 400 500 m

BERMONDSEY

© A-Z/OS

Bermondsey Antiques Market **G2**

Bermondsey Square Hotel **G2**

Bermondsey Street **G2/3**

BFI Southbank **B4**

Borough Market **E4**

Butler's Wharf **H3**

Cantina del Ponte **H3**

Chop House **H3**

City Hall **G3**

Fashion and Textile Museum **G3**

Fishcotheque **B3**

Garden Museum **A1**

Garrison, The **G3**

George Inn, The **E3**

Hay's Galleria **F4**

Hayward Gallery **B4**

Hotel ME **A5**

Imperial War Museum **C2**

Lambeth Palace **A1**

London Aquarium **A3**

London Eye **A3**

Maltby Street **G2**

Menier Chocolate Factory **E3**

Namco Funscape **A3**

Nightingale Museum **A2**

Old Operating Theatre Museum & Herb Garden **F3/4**

Old Vic Theatre **B3**

Oxo Tower **C3**

Pont de le Tour **H3**

Queen Elizabeth Hall **B4**

Royal Festival Hall **A4**

Royal National Theatre **B4**

ScooterCaffè **B2**

Shakespeare's Globe Theatre and Sam Wanamaker Playhouse **D3**

Somerset House **A5**

Southbank Centre **A3**

Southwark Cathedral **E4**

Tanner & Co **G3**

Tate Modern **D3**

The Clink Prison Museum **E4**

The Rose Exhibition **E4**

The Shard **F3**

Tower Bridge **H3/4**

Tower of London **G4**

Village East **G2**

Waterloo Bridge **A4**

Young Vic **C3**

Step on a glass walkway on London's most famous river crossing, Tower Bridge

The silhouette of **Tower Bridge** is second only to Big Ben as the most recognisable symbol of London. When it was unveiled in 1894, Tower Bridge was at the cutting edge of modern technology. Even now, watching the bridge opening up is to understand why London was once the most technologically advanced city in the world.

This suspension bridge is also equipped with a massive bascule (seesaw) mechanism that swings into life and raises the two sides of the bridge in three minutes to allow oncoming shipping through.

Although London's days as a thriving port are long gone, 40,000 people a day cross the bridge and it still lifts around 1,000 times a year. Check the website to find out when the next lifting will be – it's usually at least once a day.

You can also tour the Victorian engine rooms to see how they work, and walk the high walkways for some of the best views of the river. And now these are even better – the spectacular glass floor arrived on the high-level walkway in 2015. It's not suitable for vertigo sufferers, as you actually look 42 metres/138 ft down onto the river and traffic below.

Tower Bridge; tel: 020 7403 3761; www.towerbridge.org.uk; map H3/4

Restaurants at Butler's Wharf

On the south side of the bridge, there are plenty of choices for a great feed, all housed in a once derelict warehouse (36 Butler's Wharf). **Le Pont de la Tour** serves refined French seafood (tel: 020 7403 8403); the traditional British **Butler's Wharf Chop House** (tel: 020 7403 3403); the Italian-leaning **Cantina del Ponte** (tel: 020 7403 5403) with outdoor terraces overlooking the Thames; and lighter dishes at **Brown's Bar & Brasserie** (tel: 020 7378 1700). Map H3

Sing the praises of London's oldest Gothic building at Southwark Cathedral

It may not look much from outside, particularly in a city graced with St Paul's Cathedral and Westminster Abbey, but **Southwark Cathedral** is far more beautiful on the inside. Properly known as Cathedral and Collegiate Church of St Saviour and St Mary Overie, Southwark, this is one of London's oldest places of worship. It is believed that there has been a church on this spot for over 1,000 years, and the remains of an altar to a Roman hunter god were unearthed here in the 1970s. A fire in 1212 badly damaged the earlier Norman church, traces of which can be seen in the nave. The cathedral was then rebuilt and is now London's oldest standing Gothic building.

Southwark was the city's first theatre district, and the area's stage connections are reflected here with monuments to actors, poets and playwrights. A window in the south aisle commemorates William Shakespeare, depicting characters from all 36 of his plays. The tomb of his brother, Edmond, lies between the choir stalls. Geoffrey Chaucer's pilgrims set off from a nearby hostelry, The Tabard, in *The Canterbury Tales*.

The Tabard no longer stands, but the neighbouring **George Inn** (map E3) is still there; and as London's last remaining galleried coaching inn, it is well worth a visit (very busy with a post-work crowd).

There are music recitals almost daily. Try to catch the impressive cathedral choir in full song – there is regular choral evensong by candlelight, organ recitals and special choral concerts (check website for times).

The cathedral has an airy Refectory (open until 7pm), serving sandwiches, salads and soups plus afternoon tea.

Southwark Cathedral, Montague Close; tel: 020 7367 6700; www.cathedral. southwark.anglican.org; map E4

Head up to the top of The Shard and marvel at London's other 21st-century skyscrapers

It's hard to believe that St Paul's Cathedral was the tallest building in London, at a mere 111 metres (364 ft), until the BT Tower was built in 1962. And how the city's skyline has changed since. Completed in 2012 and designed by Renzo Piano, **The Shard** is now the tallest building in Western Europe at a sleek height of 306 metres (1004 ft), its tapering, jagged point like a shard of glass, hence the name. Even though Londoners don't usually care for modern architecture, this is one they seem to like. It has also won a slew of architectural awards.

Its 87 floors comprise a viewing platform, champagne bar, luxury hotel, restaurants and bars, with the majority of floors used as office space. It's a genuine vertical village.

Most visitors would head to this landmark building for **The View from the Shard**, the viewing platform at the top (floors 68, 69 and 72). Behind immense windows – with the very top floor open to the elements – you have spectacular 360° views across the city up to 60 km (40 miles) on a clear day. (That said, it really is advisable to wait for a clear day for your visit, as tickets aren't cheap.) If you want more information on the landmarks

you spot, the high-tech digital 'tell:scopes' allow you to find out more via the viewing screen.

The Shard isn't only about viewing. At the top, you can indulge in a yoga class (www.yogasphere.eu) or a silent disco. There are special events for Valentine's Day and Christmas. You can also head to the country's highest champagne bar.

But aside from buying a ticket to head to the top, you can part with your cash in different ways. Around midway up the floors are devoted to dining and hospitality. The **Shangri-La** hotel opened its luxurious doors

in 2015 taking up floors 34-52 and with that, its slick lounge bar **Gong**, the restaurant **Ting**, with modern European cuisine with Asian influences, and the deli and café **Lang**.

A couple of floors down are three more places to dine: **Aqua Shard** (tel: 020 3100 1256) serves contemporary British cuisine but its three-storey atrium bar is a real showstopper – it's well worth getting just a cocktail here, to gaze at the evening panorama. **Oblix** (tel: 020 7268 6700) serves Rainer Becker's contemporary European cuisine – its charcoal grill and wood-fired oven are at the heart of its kitchen. **Hutong** (tel: 020 3100 1257) is all dark and sensual, serving dishes from the imperial palaces of northern China.

This may state the obvious, but of course a table by the window is the real icing on the cake – try to request this when making your reservations!

The View From the Shard, Joiner St; tel: 0844 499 7111; www.theviewfromthe shard.com
Shanri-la Hotel, 32/F The Shard, 31 St Thomas St; tel: 020 7234 8000; www.shangri-la.com/london; map F3

Discover the delights of a Chelsea bun and other gourmet pleasures at Borough Market

On Saturday mornings, it feels like all of London – and a large chunk of the rest of the world's food-loving population – have come to **Borough Market** to wander around and chomp on a sandwich, a sausage or some other gourmet delight. Borough is London's oldest covered fruit-and-veg market, and the go-to place for top chefs in search of premium ingredients and grazers looking for tasty treats.

It's not just about the chefs, or the well-to-do foodies, buying their ingredients. The market is also a hugely popular spot for food to go and it's hard to think of anyone, however simple or exotic their tastes, going home disappointed. There are also regular kitchen demonstration sessions.

You can find everything here: artisan cheeses, cured hams, stuffed olives, truffle oil, freshly pressed juices, oysters, fish and chips, kebabs, falafels, veggie burgers, chocolates, pastries and cakes, including the eccentric British Chelsea bun and Eccles cake. Standouts (with queues) are: the chorizo sandwich at Spanish specialist stall **Brindisa**, the fish finger butties at **fish!** and the scallops and bacon at **Shellseekers**.

If you'd rather sit down, there are plenty of cafés and restaurants inside or outside the market which take most of their ingredients from the traders here. **Roast** (Stoney St; tel: 020 3006 6111) is a gorgeous restaurant in the Floral Hall specialising in roast meats and seasonal game. Take a post-lunch pick-me-up at **Monmouth Coffee Company** (2 Park St; tel: 020 7232 3010), which roasts its beans from single farms and cooperatives. Sample seafood at **Wright Brothers Oyster and Porter House** (11 Stoney St; tel: 020 7403 9554) – a long oyster bar and high tables.

Borough Market, Southwark St; lunch market Mon & Tue, full market Wed–Sat; www.boroughmarket.org.uk; map E4

Take in a living, breathing panorama on the London Eye

The **London Eye** has become a much-loved part of the landscape in a relatively short amount of time. The Eye (whose named sponsor changes every couple of years) also does the same trick as the Eiffel Tower does for Paris, to let people climb above the city and look back down on it. The London Eye was opened in 2000 as a way of celebrating the new Millennium and was only meant to be there for a few years, but its permanent status was declared soon after and it is hard to visualise the city without it. Although its height has since been surpassed by other observation wheels, this is still one of the world's largest.

Once you have climbed into your space-age steel-and-glass capsule, the wheel's graceful 30-minute revolution lets you appreciate just how big London really is, when you have the whole glorious 360-degree panorama at your feet.

Although it seems slightly kitsch in comparison, your ticket also includes admission to the 4D cinema experience, complete with 3D glasses – it's unexpectedly entertaining.

The building directly behind it is **County Hall**, once the seat of London's local government, now home to restaurants and cafés.

The London Eye; tel: 0333 321 2001; www.londoneye.com

Marvel at one of the world's most dynamic modern art spaces, Tate Modern, and its new extension

Tate Modern is an amazing story of redemption and reinvention. It resides in the former Bankside Power Station, a hulking monolith that closed in 1981 and was regarded as a monstrous blemish on the Thames skyline. After an amazing makeover by Swiss architects Herzog & de Meuron, and opened in 2000, it is universally loved as the home for the Tate's world-class collection of modern art and a hugely popular venue.

Its permanent display includes works from Matisse, Pollock and Picasso to Anish Kapoor and Tacita Dean – you name 'em, they've got 'em. You could happily spend a day exploring them all, and also find time for the latest barnstorming exhibition. The biggest, most audacious, installations are in the vast **Turbine Hall**. One of its most famous recent installations was Ai Weiwei's *Sunflower Seeds*, where he covered the entire floor with life-size handmade porcelain seeds – apparently identical yet unique. The **Material Gestures** galleries on Level 3 feature an impressive offering of post-World War II painting and sculpture. Room 7 contains a breathtaking collection of Rothkos and Monets. There are regular free 45-minute guided tours on each gallery.

A favourite among Londoners is the **restaurant** on Level 7, especially on Friday and Saturday late opening, with stunning views of the Thames and St Paul's, opposite. But that's now matched with the roof terrace on the Tate's new extension, which opened in June 2016. This ten-storey twisted, pyramid-shaped building is the same height as the existing Tate's chimneys, and has an extra 60 percent space for galleries, with live performance in the Tanks, in the basement.

Tate Modern, Bankside; tel: 020 7887 8888; www.tate.org.uk/modern; Sun–Thur 10am–6pm, Fri–Sat 10am–10pm; free; map D4

Let the players entertain you at an Elizabethan playhouse and visit Shakespeare's Globe

There wouldn't be a **Shakepeare's Globe** if it wasn't for American movie director and actor Sam Wanamaker. Wanamaker began his acting career performing Shakespeare in a replica of the Globe in Ohio. When visiting London in 1949, he was amazed to discover that there was no commemoration of the Globe so he set about getting this faithful reconstruction built close to the site of the original Elizabethan playhouse, where most of Shakespeare's plays were first performed. He raised most of the money but sadly, Wanamaker didn't live to see the Globe opened by the Queen in 1997. More than 300,000 visitors a year come to watch a play or visit the permanent exhibition depicting the Bard's life and times. In 2011 a large donation enabled the last part of Wanamaker's dream: an indoor Jacobean theatre. In 2013 the Sam Wanamaker Playhouse opened adjacent to the Globe, an intimate venue lit by beeswax candles in huge candelabras.

These two venues offer contrasting experiences, with performances at the Globe in summer months – mainly contemporary takes on Shakespearean – on its open-air stage and courtyard for the 'groundlings'. The Playhouse, next door, has year-round performances.

Shakespeare's Globe Theatre, 21 New Globe Walk; tel: 020 7902 1400; www.shakespeares-globe.org; map D4

Climb a church tower and discover the fascinating if gory surrounds of the Old Operating Theatre

chapel roof once butted on to the women's ward of St Thomas's Hospital and they were wheeled in from there. However, in 1862, the 12th-century hospital buildings were knocked down to make way for London Bridge Station, and these rooms were boarded up and totally forgotten about until their rediscovery in 1956.

You will need to steel your nerves for some of the displays of bottled organs and body parts, and the cases of instruments used by the surgeons in the Victorian operating theatre are truly scary – many of them look much better suited to torture than to healing. None of it, however, is as terrifying as the thought that, until 1847, surgeons had no anaesthesia and depended on alcohol or opiates to dull the patient's senses. The less squeamish should check for the surgery demos staged by museum staff (usually at weekends) as these are both hilarious and amazingly enlightening on history, science and human fortitude.

You need to negotiate an ancient, steep and rickety spiral staircase to get here, but this beautiful oak-beamed loft is one of London's most intriguing historical interiors. Hidden in the roof of a hospital chapel, this is the oldest surviving **operating theatre** in Europe, and don't worry, the patients didn't have to get up here this way; the

Old Operating Theatre Museum and Herb Garret, 9a St Thomas's Street; tel: 020 7188 2679; www.thegarret.org.uk; daily 10.30am–5pm; map F3–4

Eat, shop and play in London's cool destination, Bermondsey Street

Bermondsey has an edgy, undis-covered feel to it. It's an unlikely backwater of southeast London, under the railway arches, which has become a popular Saturday morning shopping hub. **Maltby Street** (pictured) is now a weekend street market and it's something of a hub for gastronomes with dozens of great food stalls. It certainly gives the much larger, older Borough Market a run for its money, with stalls ranging from Mozambique hot sauces at **African Volcano** and hand-salted smoked salmon at **Hansen & Lydersen** to homemade gin infusions at **Little Bird Gin**.

The best way of exploring it is to start in **Bermondsey Street** where you can bag hip finds from small funky shops, and eat your way round the world in stylish pubs, restaurants and bars.

Bermondsey Square is home to the area's oldest attraction, the Friday **Antiques Market** (6am–2pm), with dozens of outdoor stalls selling second-hand furniture, china and jewellery. You can pop in for breakfast at **Del'Aziz** (11 Bermonsey Square), a Moroccan-style lounge with a glass floor revealing the remains of 11th-century Bermondsey Abbey. Then, walking north towards London

Bridge you will pass: **Pure and Applied** (169), a frame store with affordable prints, photographs and maps; **Village East** (171–173), with good modern European cuisine with a natural wood interior; and **Bermond-sey 167** (167), a boutique strong on quirky homeware and jewellery. **Holly and Lil** (103) has everything for the chic city dog, with pet collars and har-nesses. **The Garrison** (99) is a relaxed and beautifully restored gastro-pub – great for Sunday lunch. **The Fashion and Textile Museum** (83), founded by Zandra Rhodes, has a striking orange and pink building and showcases fashion, jewellery and textile design. **Tanner & Co** (50) serves British com-fort food in a converted warehouse.

Bermondsey Street; map G2/3
Maltby Street; map G2

127

Experience culture high and low in the galleries and halls around the Southbank Centre

The **Southbank Centre** is a 21-acre metropolitan arts centre with an extraordinary history. It all started in 1951 with the Festival of Britain. At that time, London was badly in need of redevelopment, and the Festival was described as a tonic for the nation. Warehouses and housing were cleared to make a new public space and the Festival buildings went up. It was a resounding success, but when Churchill got back into power in 1953, his government promptly razed all but the **Royal Festival Hall** for being 'too socialist'. However over the ensuing decades other cultural halls and exhibition spaces – the Queen Elizabeth Hall, the Hayward Gallery and the Purcell Room, all of which reopen in 2017 after major renovations – were added until the Royal Festival Hall became the beating heart at the centre of the Southbank. And whatever you think of the oft-criticised brutal modernist architecture, the Southbank is still a tonic for all. With three auditoriums hosting world-class orchestras, musical ensembles and dance performances, plus cutting-edge art exhibitions and outdoor performances, it is a constant hive of activity of the highest order.

Surrounding the centre is mesmerising array of flavours: **Southbank Centre Food Market** (Fri–Sun noon–6pm) has street food and produce; the river terrace has branches of the classier fast-food chains such as Ping Pong and Le Pain Quotidien; inside the Festival Hall is **Skylon** restaurant for fine dining, the Queen Elizabeth Hall Roof Garden is a relaxing family-friendly space with spectacular views and a bar; under the railway arches is **Topolski**, an all-day café and bar built into the art studios of the late Feliks Topolski.

Next door is the **Royal National Theatre**, with its three theatres and

exciting roster of plays. If you haven't managed to get advanced tickets you could try for returns on the day, or take a behind-the-scenes tour of the three theatres. Alternatively, head outside and catch the street theatre of the skateboarding kids as they slam and pop up and down concrete steps and under the walkways.

Or walk along to the neighbouring **BFI Southbank** (home of the British Film Institute) which has four cinema screens showing everything from Charlie Chaplin to Michael Haneke and some commercial releases. BFI Southbank has a lovely relaxed café and bar, **Denugo**, with long low leather sofas, and the Thames-side **Riverfront** bar and café. There's also a fabulous shop, essential for all cinephiles. If you have spare time between screenings browse the second-hand book stall on the terrace come rain or shine.

Southbank Centre, Belvedere Road; tel: 020 7960 4200; www.southbankcentre. co.uk
Hayward Gallery, South Bank; tel: 020 7960 4200; www.hayward.org.uk; map A4
National Theatre, South Bank; tel: 020 7452 3000; www.nationaltheatre.org.uk; map B4
BFI Southbank, Belvedere Road; tel: 020 7928 3232; www.bfi.org.uk; map B4

See stage and screen stars tread the boards at The Old Vic

Many of the great names of British stage and screen – John Gielgud, Alec Guinness, Laurence Olivier, Judi Dench, Glenda Jackson, Anthony Hopkins – got their start or established their reputation at **The Old Vic**. So when, gasp, an American, the actor Kevin Spacey, was appointed artistic director in 2003 there were mixed reactions. Could a film actor, albeit such a fine one, from New Jersey really understand this revered theatre that for 200 years had been a driving force in British playmaking? His first year was shaky, but from then until he stepped down in 2015 Spacey drew in huge audiences. His overhaul included more comfortable seats and a decent bar, and introduc-

ing the Bridge Project, a scheme he hatched with Sam Mendes (formerly creative director of the Donmar Warehouse, see page 56, and now a New York-based film director) and the Brooklyn Academy of Music. The idea was to enmesh the theatrical worlds of London, Broadway and Hollywood, and the result has been a series of productions of classic texts with stellar casts.

Around the corner is the marvellous **ScooterCaffè** (132 Lower Marsh, map B2) for coffee (brewed in a retro 1957 Faema espresso machine) and beers in a scooter workshop. Across the road is **The Young Vic**, a training ground for young directors, playwrights and actors, which has a much larger, all-day café, **The Cut**. Another dynamic small theatre in the area is **The Menier Chocolate Factory**, which specialises in quirky musicals and new plays that often transfer to a West End theatre.

The Old Vic, The Cut; tel: 020 7928 2651; www.oldvictheatre.com; map B3
The Young Vic, The Cut; tel: 020 7922 2922; www.youngvic.org; map C3
Menier Chocolate Factory, 51 Southwark St; tel: 020 7378 1713; www.menier chocolatefactory.com; map E3

Tour the Imperial War Museum and discover that it is not just for gun-obsessed boys or war historians

Perhaps it is no accident that the grand structure housing the **Imperial War Museum** was once Bethlem, a hospital for the care of the insane from which the word 'bedlam' comes. For the museum is a crazy kind of place that does a marvellous job of conveying the madness of conflict, from World War I to the present day. Reopened in 2014 after a £40 million redesign, it's now better than ever. Its soaring, four-storey atrium houses the collection's huge items, and there are new First World War galleries, a contemporary art gallery and a terrace café opening onto the park.

During the week it is likely to be full of school children peering at bomber planes and crawling around reconstructed trenches. It shows how vibrant a museum can be even if it is dedicated to grim events. The Imperial War Museum has dedicated itself to living history rather than dusty cases of artefacts. So you don't just see photographs of bombed-out London streets; you can go and sit in a replica of a shelter and listen to the neighbours argue, punctuated by scarily realistic sounds of bombs falling. There are changing exhibitions covering different aspects, from espionage to classic war photography.

Imperial War Museum, Lambeth Road; tel: 020 7416 5000; www.iwm.org.uk; daily 10am–6pm; free; map C2

KENSINGTON AND CHELSEA

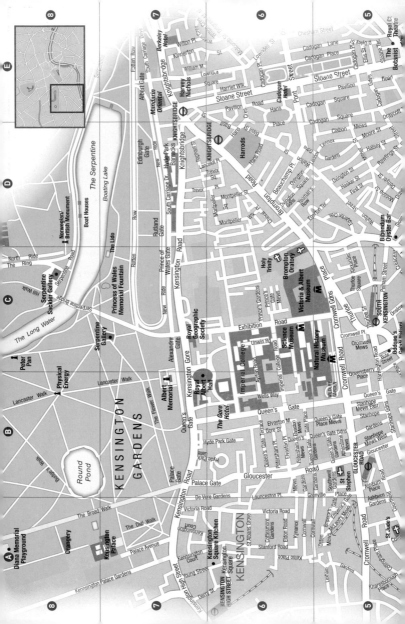

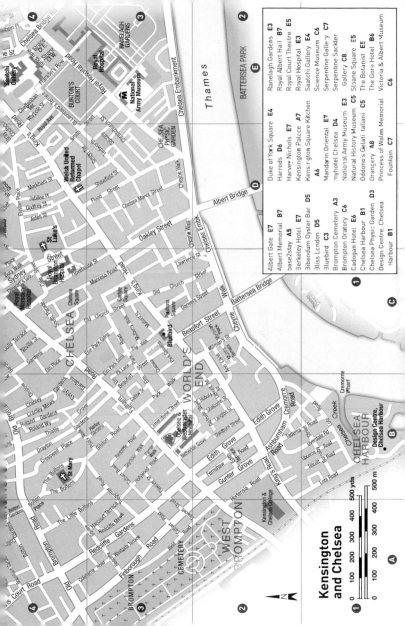

Kensington and Chelsea

Albert Gate	**E7**	
Albert Memorial	**B7**	
base2stay	**A5**	
Berkeley Hotel	**E7**	
Bibendum Oyster Bar	**D5**	
Bliss London	**D5**	
Bluebird	**C3**	
Brompton Cemetery	**A3**	
Brompton Oratory	**C6**	
Cadogan Hotel	**E6**	
Chelsea Harbour	**B1**	
Chelsea Physic Garden	**D3**	
Design Centre Chelsea Harbour	**B1**	
Duke of York Square	**E4**	
Harrods	**D6**	
Harvey Nichols	**E7**	
Kensington Palace	**A7**	
Kensington Square Kitchen	**A6**	
Mandarin Oriental	**E7**	
myhotel Chelsea	**D4**	
Natural History Museum	**E3**	
Oddono's Gelati Italiani	**C5**	
Orangery	**A8**	
Princess of Wales Memorial Fountain	**C7**	
Ranelagh Gardens	**E3**	
Royal Albert Hall	**B7**	
Royal Court Theatre	**E5**	
Royal Hospital	**E3**	
Saatchi Gallery	**E4**	
Science Museum	**C6**	
Serpentine Gallery	**C7**	
Serpentine Sackler Gallery	**C8**	
Sloane Square	**E5**	
The Botanist	**E5**	
The Gore Hotel	**B6**	
Victoria & Albert Museum	**C6**	

Shop in luxury at the iconic emporium, Harrods, and its fashionista neighbour, Harvey Nichols

Harrods has 330 departments spread over 1 million square feet, so your visit requires as much precision planning as your trip to the British Museum. List the things you most want to see and work out a circuit (the website has a floor guide, and there's also an app). Whether you are looking to buy a fossil, a dress, or a teddy bear sporting a Harrods logo sweater, you should also visit the beautiful tiled food halls, the Christmas Store (Aug–Dec) and the pet department. Its exquisite food hall (pictured) is a destination in its own right.

And make use of Harrods' cafés and restaurants – there are around 30 – to restore and re-energise as you make your way around this splendid emporium. These include elegant dining at The Georgian Restaurant, Caviar House Seafood Bar, French gourmet at Galvin Demoiselle and the Urban Retreat Café, next to the spa and salon.

Fans of *Absolutely Fabulous* will know that 'Harvey Nicks' has a near fanatical following among London's fashionistas. Much smaller than its more famous neighbour, **Harvey Nichols** is the one that Knightsbridge 'Ladies who Lunch' could not do without. It has a great beauty hall, a divine food department and good menswear and kids' departments, but its main attractions are women's fashion and accessories, both of which feature collections by hot young designers as well as elegant classics. Don't forget to admire the windows on your way in; they are cheeky and fun, and you can see Londoners on passing buses craning their necks to get a proper look at them.

CHARCUTERIE

136

Harrods, 87 Brompton Rd; tel: 020 7730 1234; www.harrods.com; Mon–Sat 10am–9pm, Sun 11.30am–6pm. map D6 Harvey Nichols, 109–125 Knightsbridge; tel: 020 7235 5000; www.harvey nichols.com; map E7. Both stores: Mon–Sat 10am–8pm, Sun 11.30am–6pm

Study Sloane Rangers close up at The Botanist, Bluebird and Bibendum Oyster Bar

A highlight of these high-end eateries is all about location, and people watching. **The Botanist** is a modern, light-filled bar but like many beloved homes, it's the feeling inside and the view *out* that are most important. The beauty of the Botanist is the ace views from its huge windows of the well-heeled people of Chelsea going about their daily shopping. It has a glorious brunch with blueberry buttermilk pancakes with streaky bacon or soft shell crab Benedict. But lunch or dinner, when the bar is full of beautiful people, are good too, with a standout apple tarte tatin for two with crème fraîche and caramel sauce.

Bluebird Café is a great meeting place, with tables in the terrace summer courtyard giving perfect ringside viewing of all the social interactions of a Chelsea weekend. The prices may reflect the chichi nature of the neighbourhood, but the Bluebird is one of the best places to meet, drink and hang a while in this neck of the woods.

The Bibendum Oyster Bar (pictured) is in a beautiful Grade II-listed tiled building, formerly the head-quarters of the French tyre company, Michelin. It recently revamped its foyer, installing two huge glass screens opening onto Fulham Road.

There is also the Crustacea Stall, adjacent to the café, where you can pick up a cooked lobster with home-made mayonnaise. Alternatively, just explore the genteel streets with an Italian ice cream from **Oddono's** (14 Bute St; tel: 020 7052 0732; map C5), which has dozens of delicious – and unusual – flavours to choose from.

The Botanist, 7 Sloane Square; tel: 020 7730 0077; map E5
Bluebird Café, 350 King's Rd; tel: 020 7559 1000; map C3
The Bibendum Oyster Bar, Michelin House, 81 Fulham Rd; tel: 020 7589 1480; map D5

Step inside the Darwin Centre's amazing high-tech Cocoon and see science in action

When the Natural History Museum opened its £78 million extension, the **Darwin Centre**, in 2009, they did it with the express purpose of inspiring the next generation of naturalists and scientists. Merely housing their collections, and the people who study them, was not enough. They wanted museum-goers to get involved and be excited by the knowledge-gathering too. And they have achieved it brilliantly. The eight-storey glass-and-steel building has a weird white cocoon (it looks as if it's about to hatch a massive bug worthy of a scary sci-fi movie) at its public point of entry. You ride a glass lift to the top and then work your way down the Cocoon's white ramps looking at everything from specimens brought back by Darwin from his first exhibition on *The Beagle* in 1831 to the latest species of lichen or dust mite to be discovered. Educators are always talking about how knowledge is power, and you really feel the buzz of it as you wander round, interacting with glass screens, watching cases of bugs or birds or berries reveal their secrets as you press buttons, and get to observe, and interact with, the white-coated scientists as they go about their researches.

Don't neglect the beautiful Victorian halls of its older sibling, **The Natural History Museum**. It has fantastic exhibits of dinosaurs and other marvellous creatures, including the dodo, and a full-size model of a blue whale. Right next door, the huge **Science Museum** has varied permanent and temporary exhibitions for all ages; the new interactive gallery has live event spaces and hands-on experiments.

The Darwin Centre, The Natural History Museum, Cromwell Road; tel: 020 7942 5000; www.nhm.ac.uk; daily 10am–5.50pm, booking required for timed slots; free; map C5
Science Museum, Exhibition Road; tel: 020 7942 4000; www.sciencemuseum.org.uk; daily 10am–6pm; free; map C6

Relish a heavenly choir in the ornate Italian Renaissance splendour of the Brompton Oratory

This flamboyant Baroque church is arguably London's most famous Catholic church, and undoubtedly the most Roman as it is an almost exact imitation of the Church of the Gesù in Rome. The Oratory also has treasures from Italy scattered around it such as the giant statues of the Twelve Apostles in the nave, which were carved from Carrara marble by Giuseppe Mazzuoli in the 1680s and brought here from Siena's cathedral when the Oratory was completed in 1884. And the magnificent Lady Altar created for the Dominican church in Brescia in 1693.

The London Oratory, or the Church of the Immaculate Heart of Mary, to give it its proper name, was the first Roman Catholic church to be built in England after the Reformation, and it still adheres to the rigid ritualised 'high' Catholicism popular in that day. Every Sunday there is a Mass sung in Latin, and while this marble-encrusted church is much admired for its architecture and elaborate painted ceiling, it is the music that's really made its name.

The Oratory has three choirs. The repertoire of the internationally renowned Choir of the London Oratory covers all periods of music from Gregorian chant to the present day, and the choir takes part in liturgies here most days. Then there is the boys-only London Oratory School Schola who perform at concerts around the city and sing at the Saturday 6pm Mass. Sweeter still is the junior choir, comprised of 8–16 year-olds from around the city, who you can catch practising after school most days of the week

The Brompton Oratory, Brompton Rd; tel. 020 7808 0900; daily 6.30am-8pm; www.bromptonoratory.co.uk; map C6

Put your feet up in the Victoria & Albert Muscum's delightful John Madejski Garden

Whatever you think of the vicissitudes of fashion, you'd have to admit that any museum that has a little black dress, as first conceived by Coco Chanel, in its permanent collection must be quite an interesting place. And the **V&A** is uniquely absorbing. Widely acclaimed as the greatest decorative arts museum in the world, it is also one of London's liveliest and most imaginative museums. In addition to its permanent collection it also hosts impressive exhibitions – its most popular (probably of all time) was David Bowie Is, an outstanding retrospective in 2013 of the great man's career.

With 7 miles of galleries to traipse around and over 4.5 million objects spread on its six floors – ceramics, furniture, fashion, glass, jewellery, photographs, sculpture, textiles, paintings – the V&A is a notoriously complicated building to navigate, so pick up a free map on your way in. Or resign yourself to the almost inevitable, and get a little lost – you never know what you'll discover.

Another option is to take a free one-hour tour (from the Meeting Point near Grand Entrance, 10.30am, 12.30pm, 1.30 & 3.30pm) to orient yourself – there are also special themed tours and talks.

Otherwise wear comfortable shoes, and make sure you don't miss the **John Madejski Garden**, a delightful courtyard where you can have a rest and a coffee or dip your throbbing toes in cool water.

Between your calming interludes in the garden, consider venturing to: the **Fashion Gallery** (Room 40), for an overview of the British contribution to fashion since the 18th century, and a collection of corsetry through the ages that will make you wince; the **British Galleries** (Rooms 52–58), devoted to British design-

ers from 1500 to 1900 and full of beautiful diversions – among them the Great Bed of Ware, mentioned in Shakespeare's *Twelfth Night*; the **Gallery of Japanese Art** (Room 44), with an eclectic collection from ornate samurai armour to a Hello Kitty rice cooker; the **Exhibition Landscape Gallery** (Room 87), with its breathtaking collection of British landscapes by Constable and Turner; the **Medieval and Renaissance Galleries** (Room 58), which includes Bernini's *Neptune with Triton*; and the **Cast Courts**, which have lite-

sized plaster models of ancient and medieval statuary and architecture including Michelangelo's *David*, and the front of Santiago de Compostela cathedral. The idea was to allow artists unable to afford a 'grand tour' of Europe the chance to draw the treasures. It is to this day full of people sketching away. Don't be shy: bring a pad and have a doodle yourself.

Victoria & Albert Museum, Cromwell Rd; tel: 020 7942 2000; www.vam.ac.uk; daily 10am–5.45pm, Fri until 10pm; free; map C6

Get some interior inspiration at the Design Centre Chelsea Harbour

Ever secretly thought if you could live your life over again you'd be an interior designer and swish about with swatches of fabric, testing feather beds and choosing chandeliers? Well, the **Design Centre Chelsea Harbour** is the place to live out that fantasy. Once open only to architects and decorators, it's now open to the public. And very impressive it is too, with its three glass domes and immense black olive trees over which swoop graceful swans coming in to land. In the 105 showrooms you can find all the things you could need to create every style of your dream home. You could source lamps with duck feet in the Porta Romana shop, or handcrafted English lighting – which has supplied luxury hotels and royal residences the world over – from Besselik & Jones. You could even deck out that fantasy yacht here too (if walking round the harbour outside has given you boat envy). More prosaically you could just pick up some colour charts if you are thinking of repainting the kitchen, find out who makes the deepest sofa or the plushest carpet or treat yourself to a new bedside lamp, cushion, tea cup or bath mat.

The **Design Café** in the North Dome has hearty food, from homemade cakes to Thai green curry, in suitably designery surroundings or there's the nearby **Lots Road bar and restaurant** (114 Lots Rd) for a nice laidback Bloody Mary, Sunday lunch or bar snack.

The Design Centre, Chelsea Harbour; tel: 020 7225 9166; www.dcch.co.uk; Mon–Fri 9.30am–5.30pm; map B1

Attend a concert in the Royal Albert Hall – one of the world's most elegant auditoriums

The **Royal Albert Hall** is not quite the thing of magnificent beauty originally planned by Prince Albert, Queen Victoria's consort. He wanted a hall that seated 30,000, but his death from typhoid meant that a large part of the funds, donated by the public, were diverted to creating his memorial statue. A gilded statue of Albert now sits in his memorial facing the Royal Albert Hall in Kensington Gardens, spectacularly lit at night, and his architects were left to continue with the domed concert hall inspired by Roman amphitheatres. If Albert could see it now, even though it was scaled down to seat 7,000, he would almost certainly be delighted with the breadth of its reach – Wagner, Verdi and Elgar conducted the first UK performance of their own works here, and every major classical solo artist and leading orchestra has performed here, as have light entertainment, pop and rock artists including Liza Minnelli, Jimi Hendrix, Kaiser Chiefs and the Killers. The hall is best known for the summer Proms, a series of BBC-sponsored classical concerts which provide a rich diet of affordable music. If you haven't bought a ticket, you can turn up on the day and queue up for a £5 ticket to stand in the arena or the upper galleries.

Royal Albert Hall, Kensington Gore; tel: 020 7589 8212; www.royalalberthall.com; map B7

Strike a pose in the sculpture garden of the Serpentine Gallery

In the south-eastern corner of Kensington Gardens, the **Serpentine Gallery** is a dynamic exhibition space for contemporary art, much-loved by Londoners. Each summer, the gallery doubles in size and adds another structure, thanks to the summer pavilion project; it commissions a famous international architect who has not, as yet, built in Britain, to create a 'temporary wing'. The pavilion stands from June to September and passers-by can whiz through it on their morning jog or take part in Park Nights events.

Also at the Serpentine Gallery is the sculpture garden on surrounding lawn, including a tribute to Princess Diana (see box), the gallery's former patron. Poet and artist Ian Hamilton Finlay created eight benches, a tree-plaque, and a carved stone circle.

A short walk away on the opposite side of the lake is the new **Serpentine Sackler Gallery**. Also hosting contemporary art exhibitions, it's part a classic 19th-century brick structure, and a contemporary extension designed by Zaha Hadid.

Serpentine Gallery, Kensington Gardens; map C7; Serpentine Sackler Gallery, West Carriage Drive; map C7
Both venues tel: 020 7402 6075;
www.serpentinegalleries.org; tel: 020 7402 6075; daily 10am–6pm, free

Memorials to 'Lady Di'

If you are in the mood to pay tribute to 'the people's princess' there is: **Diana, Princess of Wales Memorial Fountain** (map C7) where you can dip your toes in cool flowing water; and **Diana, Princess of Wales Memorial Playground** (map A8) which, with its sand pits, pirate ship, tepees and tree houses, is very much fun. **Kensington Palace** (www.hrp.org.uk/KensingtonPalace; map A7) has a display of the gowns that she wore on state occasions. **Diana Princess of Wales, Memorial Walk** (www.royalparks.org.uk) is for the more energetic; this 7-mile walk is easy to follow thanks to the 90 plaques set in the ground, and takes in all the London buildings and places associated with Princes William and Harry's mum.

Take afternoon tea in the courtly splendour of the Orangery, Kensington Palace

Kensington Palace was initially a country house adapted for royal use by Sir Christopher Wren. It housed the courts of William II, Queen Anne, George I and George II, and was *the* London Palace until it was usurped by the bigger, flashier, Buckingham Palace. More recently it was a much-loved home to the late Princesses Margaret and Diana. Whether you opt to tour the house or not, you would be missing a treat if you didn't have breakfast, lunch or tea in the Orangery, a magnificent 18th-century building. The Orangery has a glorious setting inside the Palace grounds, giving you time and space to soak up the quintessentially English atmosphere and the lovely views of both the palace and the sunken gardens. Formidable white Corinthian pillars and marble statues lend

the room a certain grandeur, while the piles of tempting own-made cakes can almost make you feel at home. The signature Orangery cake has a devoted following and is subject of much recipe guessing. A contender for best slice of London cake, it has a hit of sunny orange glow in every bite.

If, however, you find yourself in need of picking up or cooling down again after your visit to the Orangery, consider a quick detour to **Kensington Square Kitchen** (9 Kensington Square; tel: 020 7938 2598; map A6) for a very good cup of coffee.

The Orangery, Kensington Palace, Kensington Gardens; tel: 020 3166 6113; www.orangerykensingtonpalace.co.uk; daily, Mar–Oct 10am–6pm, Nov–Feb 10am–5pm; map A8

Make like Charles Saatchi and collect art, even if it is just on a T-shirt, at the Saatchi Gallery

British critics have often been snooty about the **Saatchi Gallery**, but to the average gallery-goer, it is actually a really nice place to look at art. Housed in the grand, 70,000 square feet of what was formerly the Duke of York's Barracks, the Saatchi has no rope barriers, the works are given lots of space and light. The walls are an unvarying shade of cream, the floors are uniform expanses of Danish pine and there are plenty of places to sit. The regularly-changing exhibitions are of contemporary artists from around the world, often who have never before exhibited in Britain.

However another reason to visit the Saatchi is the shop, with a fantastic selection of art T-shirts and exciting contemporary jewellery.

The **Gallery Mess** café-bar has exposed brickwork and vaulted ceilings – plus an alfresco terrace – and also displays art as well as serving platters of cheese and charcuterie, afternoon and weekend brunch. If you feel beholden to get involved with the art, apply to upload your work which, if selected, will be displayed on the high-res screen on the second floor, and will rotate randomly. Those who have always said modern art was so simple, a child of five could do it, may be given pause for thought by this exercise.

The Saatchi Gallery, Duke of York's HQ, King's Road; tel: 020 7811 3085; www.saatchi-gallery.co.uk; daily 10am–6pm; free; map E4

Lift your spirits in the Blue Bar at the Berkeley Hotel and other plush haunts

The area has some of the plushest bars in London, where extravagant drinks are mixed in decadent surroundings.

It is hard to say exactly why the **Blue Bar at the Berkeley Hotel** is so gorgeous. Perhaps it's the shade of peregrine blue so beloved of English country homes, or the friendly staff at beckoning distance without seeming to hover or be ingratiating. Is it the inventive list of cocktails including the showy Manhattan, and the delicious free little dishes of nuts or biscuits? Whatever it is, this is the perfect place for a quiet tête-a-tête or a little discreet celebrity-watching.

It's not far to the **Mandarin Bar** in the über-chic Mandarin Oriental Hotel, an upmarket London nightspot with contemporary décor. It's very popular with the well-heeled who frequent the area, and there are plenty of vintage champagnes and classic cocktails on the menu.

At first glance **Bar 190** looks like your average hotel bar, but there's something very rock 'n' roll about it. Perhaps that is because it was the setting of the Rolling Stones film *Beggars Banquet*. More likely it's because it is the scene of many an after-party for musicians, and

their hangers-on, who have performed at the Royal Albert Hall.

Away from the rock 'n' roll lifestyle, it's more a classic English private club feel at **The Library Bar** at the Lanesborough Hotel. Bookcases with handsome leather-bound tomes and wing chairs provide the distinguished atmosphere – its vintage cognacs dating from the 1770s are legendary.

Blue Bar at the Berkeley Hotel, Wilton Place; tel: 020 7235 6000; www.the-berkeley.co.uk; map E7
Mandarin Oriental Hotel, 66 Knightsbridge; tel: 020 7201 3724; www.mandarinoriental.com; map E7
Bar 190, The Gore Hotel, 190 Kensington Gate; tel: 020 7584 6601; map B6
Lanesborough Hotel, Hyde Park Corner; tel: 020 7259 5599; www.lanesborough.com; map page 26 B2

A day of luxury and relaxation at the Mandarin Oriental Spa

The mood at the **Mandarin Oriental Spa** is as calm and Zen as the countenance of a Buddhist monk. Spread over two floors, it is all tea lights, fresh orchids, rainforest-hot steam rooms and chiming Tibetan cymbals (they mark the beginning and end of each treatment). Most of the treatments are Eastern in origin, focusing on chakras and with full body treatments, detox or facials. There are some specifically for men, such as the power left facial and therapeutic massage. There are also vitality pools and amethyst crystal steam rooms. Between times you can sip juice or a herbal tea in the Zen Relaxation Area with colour therapy lights to further soothe your nerves, all ensuring that when you come out you will feel as smooth, burnished and golden as a statue of the Buddha.

The Spa at Mandarin Oriental, 66 Knightsbridge; tel: 020 7838 9888; www.mandarinoriental.com/london; map E7

Great spa experiences in London

The Berkeley Spa (Wilton Place; tel: 020 7235 6000; map E7) is arguably London's most glamorous spa, with its rooftop pool overlooking Hyde Park and fabulous treatments. **Agua at the Sanderson** (50 Berners St; tel: 020 7300 1414; map page 80, B2) for the most luxurious futurist feel; **Kensington Day Spa** (Kensington Leisure Centre; Silchester Rd; tel: 020 3793 8220) is a low-cost alternative to plush hotels, with a session from just £15.

Check out the year-round herb and flower show at Chelsea Physic Garden

Step inside the walls of the **Chelsea Physic Garden** and three things happen in quick succession: the noise of the main road and the city disappears, your senses are assailed by the tangled fragrances of many plants and herbs, and you realise that, pretty as it is, this is no ordinary garden – this is a garden with another purpose than just being pretty. Founded in 1673 as a botanical education centre, the plants grown here have changed the course of nations: rubber plants from here went to Malaysia, and tea trees (thanks to seeds gathered in China) went to India. The garden has also changed lives: they grow around 4,000 different plants, including opium poppies, and Pacific Yew, the bark of which contains taxol, an effective drug used in the treatment of breast cancer. The Chelsea Physic Garden also boasts Britain's largest olive tree and the world's northernmost outdoor grapefruit tree. Children seem particularly to love the scary collection of carnivorous plants in one of the greenhouses. It has a special opening for Snowdrop Days (when the café and shop are open, which it doesn't usually in winter months), when these delicate win-

ter flowers bloom for two weeks, usually in January.

The café, open from Wednesday to Sunday, serves good food and on a nice day you can carry your cups of tea out into the garden, or bring a picnic and sit on one of the benches scattered throughout this fragrant haven.

Chelsea Physic Garden, 66 Royal Hospital Rd; tel: 020 7352 5646; www.chelseaphysic garden.co.uk; Apr–Oct Wed–Fri, Sun noon–5pm;Nov–Mar 10am–dusk, shop & café closed; map D3

149

VILLAGE LONDON

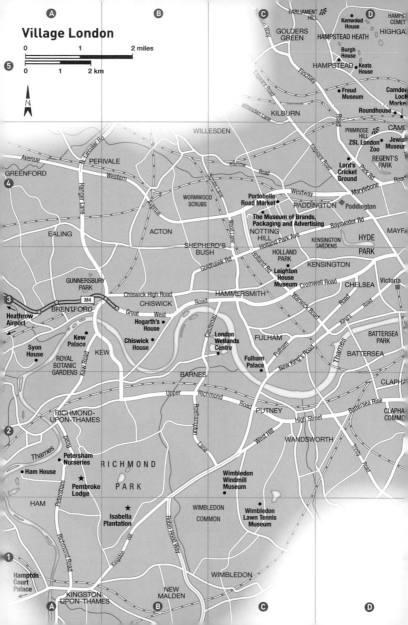

Village London

<table>
<tr><td>0</td><td>1</td><td>2 miles</td></tr>
<tr><td>0</td><td>1</td><td>2 km</td></tr>
</table>

N

A **B** **C** **D**

1 **2** **3** **4** **5**

PARLIAMENT HILL

GOLDERS GREEN

Kenwood House

HAMPSTEAD HEATH

HAMPS CEMET

HIGHGA

Burgh House

HAMPSTEAD

Keats House

Finchley

Edgware Road

Freud Museum

Camden Lock Marke

Willesden Lane

KILBURN

Roundhouse

CAM

PRIMROSE HILL

ZSL London Zoo

Jewish Museu

WILLESDEN

REGENT'S PARK

Lord's Cricket Ground

Regent's Park Rd

Rd

Edgware Road

Avenue

Larch Road

PERIVALE

Western

Harrow

Road

Westway

Marylebone

GREENFORD

Hanger Lane

Scrubs Lane

WORMWOOD SCRUBS

Portobello Road Market

PADDINGTON

Paddington

MAYF

EALING

Avenue

ACTON

SHEPHERD'S BUSH

The Museum of Brands, Packaging and Advertising

Bayswater Rd

NOTTING HILL

Holland Park Ave

KENSINGTON GARDENS

HYDE PARK

Wood Lane

Goldhawk Rd

HOLLAND PARK

Holland Rd

KENSINGTON

GUNNERSBURY PARK

Chiswick High Road

HAMMERSMITH

Road

Leighton House Museum

Cromwell Road

CHELSEA

Victoria

BRENTFORD

M4

CHISWICK

Great West

Warwick Road

King's

Road

Road

BATTERSEA PARK

Heathrow Airport

Hogarth's House

Road

London Wetlands Centre

Talgarth

FULHAM

Fulham

New King's Road

BATTERSEA

Kew Palace

Chiswick House

Fulham Palace

Thames

CLAPHA

Syon House

KEW

Kew Road

BARNES

ROYAL BOTANIC GARDENS

Upper

Richmond

Road

PUTNEY

High Street

Battersea Rise

CLAPHA COMMO

RICHMOND-UPON-THAMES

Richmond Lane

Roehampton Lane

West Hill

WANDSWORTH

Trinity Road

Thames

Petersham Nurseries

RICHMOND

PARK

Wimbledon Windmill Museum

Ham House

Petersham Road

Pembroke Lodge

HAM

Richmond Road

Isabella Plantation

Kingston Hill

WIMBLEDON COMMON

WIMBLEDON

Wimbledon Lawn Tennis Museum

Beverley Way

Hampton Court Palace

KINGSTON-UPON-THAMES

NEW MALDEN

WIMBLEDON

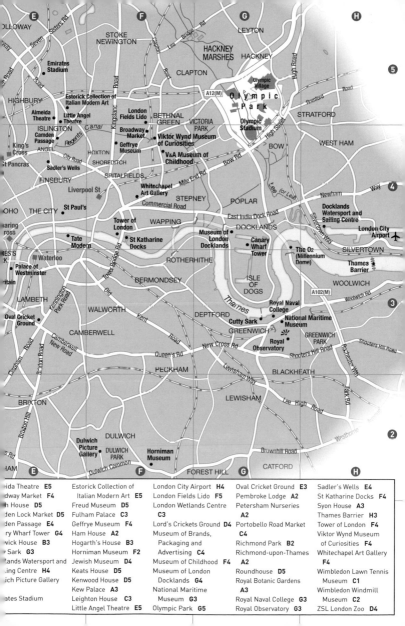

E · F · G · H

5

OLLOWAY — Seven Sisters Rd — Sisters Rd — STOKE NEWINGTON — Lea Bridge Rd — LEYTON — HACKNEY MARSHES — HACKNEY — CLAPTON — Olympic Village — Olympic Park — A12(M) — Romford Road — STRATFORD — Lee (or Lea) — High Street — WEST HAM

Emirates Stadium

HIGHBURY — Estorick Collection of Italian Modern Art — Little Angel Theatre — London Fields Lido — BETHNAL GREEN — VICTORIA PARK — Olympic Stadium — BOW

Almeida Theatre

ISLINGTON — Camden Passage — ANGEL — Broadway Market — HOXTON — Geffrye Museum — SHOREDITCH — Viktor Wynd Museum of Curiosities — V&A Museum of Childhood — Bow Rd

King's Cross — Regents — City Road

St Pancras — Sadler's Wells — FINSBURY — SPITALFIELDS — Mile End Road — STEPNEY — East India Dock Road — POPLAR — Newham — Way

4

SOHO — THE CITY — St Paul's — Liverpool St — Whitechapel Art Gallery — Commercial Road — DOCKLANDS — Docklands Watersport and Sailing Centre — London City Airport

aring cross

HES'S K — Waterloo — Tower of London — WAPPING — Museum of London Docklands — Canary Wharf Tower — The O2 (Millennium Dome) — SILVERTOWN

Palace of Westminster — Tate Modern — St Katharine Docks — ROTHERHITHE — ISLE OF DOGS — Thames Barrier — WOOLWICH

ritain — LAMBETH — Kennington Park Road — BERMONDSEY — Thames — A102(M) — Woolwich Rd

3

Oval Cricket Ground — WALWORTH — Kent Road — DEPTFORD — Royal Naval College — National Maritime Museum — GREENWICH PARK — Shooters Hill Road

CAMBERWELL — Camberwell New Road — Cutty Sark — GREENWICH — Royal Observatory

PECKHAM — Queen's Rd — New Cross Rd — Lewisham Way — BLACKHEATH

BRIXTON — Brixton Hill — LEWISHAM — Lee High Road — Park Rd

2

DULWICH — Dulwich Picture Gallery — DULWICH PARK — Horniman Museum — Brownhill Road — CATFORD

HAM — Dulwich Common — FOREST HILL

E · F · G · H

Ride the tube to Notting Hill for its antiques and chic boutiques, then relax in the Holland Park oasis

Walking around **Notting Hill** (map C4; tube: Ladbroke Grove, Notting Hill Gate) with its chichi shops, cool bars and trendy, well-heeled residents, you would never guess that, as recently as the 1960s, this was one of London's most poverty-stricken areas. Or that, in the 1950s it gave rise to Britain's first race riots when white Teddy boys clashed with incoming Caribbean residents. That is all in the past, although the Caribbean tradition is still proudly celebrated annually with the **Notting Hill Carnival** (August bank holiday weekend).

The two biggest attractions are **Portobello Road** (www.portobello road.co.uk) and Holland Park. The former bursts into life as an antiques market on Saturday (8am–6pm), but week-round has many fantastic little antique shops and boutiques for vintage (and vintage-inspired) clothes. There are also some great cafés, including **Café Garcia** (246) – also a Spanish food store – where the gazpacho is as good as any in Spain. On Sundays there is an open-air vintage market at Portobello Green.

The Museum of Brands, Packaging and Advertising (111-117 Lancaster Rd, tel: 020 7243 9611; www.museumofbrands.com) is a museum devoted to social ephemera where you can take a trip down memory lane and reconnect with all the long-forgotten packaging of your favourite childhood treats. Since 2015, when it moved to larger premises, it has a Time Tunnel exhibition space and capsule Time Line.

Holland Park (map C3; tube: Holland Park) is a grand oasis of green space where you really feel you are in the countryside. At its southern end, **Leighton House Museum** (12 Holland Park Rd; tel: 020 7602 3316; www.rbkc.gov.uk/museums) was the home and studio of Victorian artist Frederic, Lord Leighton, with outstanding Arabic mosaics, while the landscaped **Kyoto Garden** has Japanese plants and water features.

Immerse yourself in the Camden market and music scene, then walk the canal path to Regent's Park

With a whopping 10 million visitors a year, **Camden Market** (map D5; tube: Camden Town, Chalk Farm) is one of London's biggest attractions, a huge sprawl of six markets from Camden to Chalk Farm. Quantity has perhaps brought with it a dilution of quality, and it has become increasingly gentrified over the years, but there are still some great finds, especially around Stables Market (towards the direction of Chalk Farm). Many of the shops and stalls are open daily, although it is busiest on Sundays.

But there's a lot more to the neighbourhood than its market. Camden has long been the spiritual home of London's music scene. Among the best venues are: **The Roundhouse** (Chalk Farm Rd) with its eclectic mix of concerts and performance, indie bar **The Barfly** (49 Chalk Farm Rd), which is credited with having launched loads of successful bands, including The Strokes and Coldplay, the **Jazz Café** (5 Parkway), a top venue for soul and R&B, and **Dublin Castle** (94 Parkway), where Madness started out, has several live unsigned bands each night.

Some of London's most valuable property is in backstreet Camden, and a stroll down the Regent's Canal allows you to peek into some very grand gardens. Following the canal heading west from the market takes you to **Regent's Park** (map D4) within about 15 minutes. The park is another huge draw with its gently sloping lawns, rose gardens and football pitches, and the **ZSL London Zoo** (tel: 020 7722 3333; www.zsl.org) – its latest attraction is the lion enclosure.

Cross Prince Albert Road, and you are in genteel **Primrose Hill** park (map D4). Climb the hill for its beautiful views back down over the whole city, and explore **Regent's Park Road**, which is lined with chic shops and great cafés.

Shop and socialise in elegant Islington, one of the capital's favourite drinking and dining spots

Now considered fairly central, **Islington** (map E4/5; tube: Angel) was built in the 19th century as one of London's first suburbs; it has some of the city's most elegant late Georgian and early Victorian squares, including the neo-Gothic **Lonsdale Square** which is worth a detour with its beautiful gardens in the centre.

Upper Street, the area's main thoroughfare, is one of London's better high streets, with lots of interesting independent shops among the more obvious chain names. Antique lovers throng to

Camden Passage on Wednesdays and Saturdays for the market. There's a popular independent cinema, **Screen on the Green** (83), and great cafés, like the **Euphorium Bakery** (202) with an onsite café, **Ottolenghi** (287), pictured, for delicious Middle Eastern-influenced Mediterranean dishes, or **Gallipolli Café Bistro** (102) for eating Turkish meze in a party atmosphere.

Islington is also the capital's alternative theatre land, with more stage space per capita than any other part of London. **Sadler's Wells** (Rosebery Ave; tel: 020 7863 8000; www.sadlerswells.com) is London's 'dance house'. The **King's Head** (115 Upper St; 020 7226 8561; www.kingsheadtheatre.com) was the first pub theatre opened since Shakespeare's day and launched the careers of Hugh Grant and Alan Rickman. There is also the **Almeida** (Almeida St; tel: 020 7359 4404; www.almeida.co.uk), one of London's most innovative small theatres, which has a great French restaurant and bar attached, and the **Little Angel Theatre** (14 Dagmar Passage; tel: 020 7226 1787; www.littleangeltheatre.com), where children are mesmerised by amazing puppet shows.

Survey the contemporary art scene, then join the Shoreditch and Hoxton lounge lizards

The postcodes E1 and E2 have the highest concentration of artists in Europe, and **Shoreditch and Hoxton** (map F4) are a thriving cultural quarter. Many people come for the galleries, but more flock here for the nightlife. Here are some of its highlights:

Galleries
Victoria Miro (16 Wharf Rd; tel: 020 7336 8109), an elegantly converted warehouse. **Parasol Unit** (14 Wharf Rd; tel: 020 7490 7373) is a swanky, not-for-profit space with first-rate exhibitions. Redchurch Street has many tiny art spaces that come and go. The fantastic old-style London pub **The Owl & the Pussycat** (34) is a more permanent fixture on this street.

Cafés, Bars, Restaurants
Kingsland Road is the way to go for fantastic cheap Vietnamese food, including **Song Que** (134) and **Mien Tay** (122). **The Breakfast Club** (2–4 Rufus St) is for all-day English and American breakfast. **Boxpark** (2–10 Bethnal Green Rd) is a pop-up but seems like a long-term fixture – a hip hangout although the range of drinks (bottled lagers) is limited.

Live Music
Rich Mix (35 Bethnal Green Rd) has live music and performance from around the world. **Hoxton Square Bar & Kitchen** has sourdough pizzas and cocktails, and live bands on their basement stage; **Calloor Callay** (65 Rivington St) is a cocktail bar and also stages gigs on its tiny stage.

A Museum and a Market
Visit **The Geffrye Museum** (136 Kingsland Rd; tel: 020 7739 9893; www.geffrye-museum.org), a series of rooms decorated in popular styles from 1600 to the present day, set out in elegant 18th-century almshouses.

On Saturdays, try **Broadway Market** (London Fields) for vintage clothes and artisan food.

Discover the revamped East End with the Olympic Park

The term 'East End' refers to the area extending out north and east from the old walled City of London. To Londoners, 'East End' used to conjure up images of chirpy cockneys, gritty dockland locations and associations with poverty and immigration. But that is now far from the whole story, and the entire area has benefitted from regeneration and hipness radiating outwards from Hoxton and Shoreditch (see page 157). The biggest news by far in the East End – in fact for the whole of the city in recent decades – was the London 2012 Olympic and Paralympic Games. The **Queen Elizabeth Olympic Park** in Stratford was the focal point of the sporting events,

and it altered the face of this traditionally deprived part of town, by building and completely landscaping derelict wasteland.

One of the key points of winning the Olympic bid was the concept of Legacy – a promise that the benefits of making the city more sporting did not start and finish with the games in the summer of 2012. Whether it has turned London into a city of sporting talent is arguable, but what is certain is that many of the venues specially built are now open to the public. These include Zaha Hadid's splendid **Aquatic Centre**, which is

East End museums

Two East End museums worth an excursion are the **V&A Museum of Childhood** (Cambridge Heath Rd; tel: 020 8983 5200; www.vam.ac.uk/moc; tube: Bethnal Green; map F4), a family favourite with toys from the near and distant past. A quirky venue is the **Viktor Wynd Museum of Curiosities** (11 Mare St; tel: 020 7998 3617; www.thelasttuesdaysociety.org; rail: Cambridge Heath; map F4) is part cocktail bar and part private collection of oddities.

now run as a public swimming pool – including the diving training pool used now by Olympic champion Tom Daley. You can try your hand at track cycling at the **Lee Valley VeloPark** in the iconic velodrome where Sir Chris Hoy and the rest of Team GB won their gold medals, or cheer on the London Lions basketball team at the **Copper Box Arena**. From 2016 the main **Olympic Stadium** has been leased by West Ham United, the English premier league football club, where they play all their home games. In addition to the sporting venues, you can also ascend the **ArcelorMittal Orbit** (http://arcelor mittalorbit.com) – the red twisting viewing tower created by Anish Kapoor. Choose your descent – by life, stairs, abseil or even a huge slide, circling the outside.

The Olympic Park is also much loved as a beautiful green space, with wild flowers, gentle hills, walkways and open spaces for public events. There are regular free tours of the site.

Queen Elizabeth Olympic Park, Stratford; tel: 0800 0722 110; http://queenelizabeth olympicpark.co.uk; map G5

Retreat to the royal gardens of Kew and Richmond where the banks of the Thames turn rural

Ever wondered what else the architects of the London Eye have done for London? Well hop on board the first boat, bus or train to Kew and see the stairway to heaven they've built at **Kew Gardens** (map A3; tube/train: Kew Gardens). The Rhizotron and Xstrata Treetop Walkway takes you 18 metres (60ft) up in the air to stroll among tree tops. It's breathtaking, as is the rest of the Royal Botanic Gardens; the largest living plant collection in the world where you can delight at the towering tropical plants of the

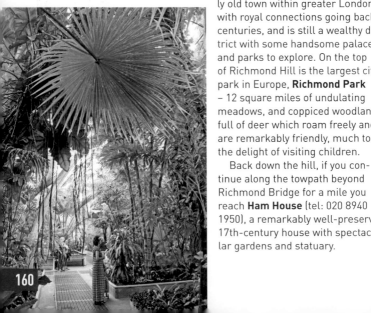

Palm House (pictured) and ascend the Chinese pagoda.

Kew is approximately 10 km (6 miles) from central London, and here the Thames is a tamer, prettier, almost bucolic thing, making this one of the best places for a river walk. The 5-km (3-mile) stretch between Kew Bridge and Richmond Bridge allows you to look in the gardens, and the Old Deer Park and gives beautiful views across the river.

Richmond-upon-Thames (map A2; tube/train: Richmond) is a love-ly old town within greater London, with royal connections going back centuries, and is still a wealthy dis-trict with some handsome palaces and parks to explore. On the top of Richmond Hill is the largest city park in Europe, **Richmond Park** – 12 square miles of undulating meadows, and coppiced woodland full of deer which roam freely and are remarkably friendly, much to the delight of visiting children.

Back down the hill, if you con-tinue along the towpath beyond Richmond Bridge for a mile you reach **Ham House** (tel: 020 8940 1950), a remarkably well-preserved 17th-century house with spectacu-lar gardens and statuary.

Stroll, swim or skate on Hampstead Heath and go on the trail of its illustrious former residents

Between the exclusive villages of Hampstead and Highgate is the marvellous verdant sprawl of **Hampstead Heath** (map D5; tube: Hampstead) – 320 hectares of woodlands, hills and ponds. The top of **Parliament Hill** has benches conveniently placed to sit and gaze out over the panorama of London or the kite flyers and dog walkers all around. Sporty types should head for one of the three **bathing ponds** – men's, women's or mixed – for a dip. And arty types should go to **Kenwood House** (tel: 0370 333 1181; www.english-heritage.org.uk; tube Archway/Golder's Green, then 210 bus), a neoclassical mansion that has Henry Moore and Barbara Hepworth statues in its grounds.

Over the years, Hampstead was known as an area for intellectuals, and there are house museums to pay tribute to its most illustrious former residents. At the **Freud Museum** (20 Maresfield Gardens; tel: 020 7435 2002; www.freud.org. uk; tube: Finchley Road) you can see the great analyst's preserved study including his couch – though not lie on it. **Keat's House** (Keats Grove; tel: 020 7332 3868; www. cityoflondon.gov.uk; tube: Hampstead Heath), pictured, is the elegant Regency villa where Keats wrote odes and fell in love with his neighbour, Fanny Browne. And **Karl Marx** is laid to rest in **Highgate Cemetery** (http://highgate cemetery.org; tube: Highgate) – 20 wild and atmospheric hectares full of dramatic and ornate Victorian graves and sombre tombs.

Both Highgate and Hampstead villages are dotted with lovely old pubs, including the allegedly haunted **Spaniards Inn** (Spaniards Road), and **The Flask** (Highgate West Hill), which has a big front garden and good Sunday lunches.

Be seduced by two handsome south London suburbs – historic Greenwich and leafy Dulwich

The importance of **Greenwich** (DLR/train: Greenwich; map G3) stretches further back in time than the Middle Ages. On the south bank of the Thames, the ancient village was the gateway between London and the Channel ports. By the 18th century the combination of Britain's wealth, maritime power and scientific learning had blessed Greenwich with the most beautiful ensemble of buildings in the British Isles.

The most spectacular way to visit Greenwich is by boat (www.dlrlondon.co.uk or www.thamesriverservices.co.uk). This way you can begin your Greenwich trip at the riverfront, gazing at the Baroque splendour of the raised colonnades and twin domes of Sir Christopher Wren's **Royal Naval College** framing the elegant simplicity of the **Queen's House**, designed by Inigo Jones in 1616. Next door, the **National Maritime Museum** (www.rmg.co.uk; tel: 020 8858 4422) displays

an unrivalled collection of maritime art and artefacts. Its 16 galleries are set around Neptune Courtyard, a spectacular space, spanned by a glass roof. The oldest of England's royal parks, the vast and glorious **Greenwich Park** dates from 1433, when the Duke of Gloucester, King Henry V's brother, created it.

Walk up the hill from the museum and you reach its most famous building, the **Royal Observatory** (www.rmg.co.uk; tel: 020 8858 4422)

Here you can stand astride the **Prime Meridian line**, a brass rail set in concrete that allows you to have one foot in the western hemisphere and the other in the eastern.

The heart of Greenwich lies just west of the park. Here you'll find the clipper ship the **Cutty Sark**, beautifully restored after a fire in 2007, Hawksmoor's **St Alfege's Church**, and **Greenwich Market** (Thur–Sun), full of little arts and crafts and food stalls.

Royal Hill is a lovely Georgian street with a gorgeous old pub, **Richard 1st** (52 Royal Hill), at one end and a good Mediterranean restaurant, **The Hill**, at the other (89).

Another historic south London suburb, often overlooked, **Dulwich** (the 'w' is silent) is also packed with interesting historic places. **Dulwich Park** (College Rd) has magnificent old oak trees and a large lake. **The Dulwich Picture Gallery** (7 Gallery Rd; www.dulwichpicturegallery.org.uk; tel: 020 8693 5254; train: West Dulwich) has a superb collection of Baroque paintings. **The Horniman Museum** (100 London Rd; www.horniman.ac.uk; tel: 020 8699 1872; train: Forest Hill) is a truly eccentric museum with an aquarium and a small children's zoo, all of which is set in a hilly park.

ESSENTIALS

A

AIRPORTS AND ARRIVAL (SEE ALSO PUBLIC TRANSPORT)

London has two major international airports: Heathrow, 15 miles (24km) to the west, and Gatwick, 25 miles (40km) to the south, plus three smaller airports, Stansted and Luton to the north and London City to the east.

Heathrow: The fastest connection to central London is the Heathrow Express (tel: 0345 600 1515; www. heathrowexpress.com) to Paddington station, which runs every 15 minutes between around 5am and 11.45pm, taking 15 minutes. Paddington then connects with several tube lines. A cheaper option is the 25-minute Heathrow Connect service (tel: 03457 000 125; www.heathrowconnect.com). There is a direct tube route on the Piccadilly line, which reaches central London in 50 minutes, via Kensington and Piccadilly to King's Cross, and operates daily from 5am (6am on Sun) until 11.40pm.

National Express (tel: 08717 818 181; www.nationalexpress.com) runs coaches from Heathrow's central bus station to Victoria Coach Station; journey time 45–80 minutes.

Gatwick: Gatwick Express (tel: 0345 850 1530; www.gatwickexpress.com) leaves Gatwick for Victoria Station every 15 minutes, 4.35am–1.35am. It takes 30 minutes. You can also take non-express services to Victoria and King's Cross, which are a bit cheaper and take 35–45 minutes.

National Express runs coaches from Gatwick's bus station to Victoria Coach Station; journey time around 90 minutes. Information, as above.

Stansted: The Stansted Express (tel: 0800 028 2878; www.stanstedexpress. com) direct rail link goes to Liverpool Street Station every 15 minutes; average journey time 45 minutes.

National Express runs coaches from Stansted to Oxford Street and Victoria Coach Station; journey time around 90 minutes. Information, as above.

London City: The DLR stop for London City Airport is six minutes from Canning Town tube (Jubilee line), running every 10 minutes from 5.30am–1.15am.

Luton: Luton Airport Parkway rail is linked by Thameslink services to King's Cross and Blackfriars, taking 40 minutes and running around every 15 minutes on weekdays only.

National Express runs coaches from Luton to Oxford Street and Victoria Coach Station; journey time around 90 minutes. Information, as above.

Airport numbers

Heathrow, tel: 0844 335 1801
Gatwick, tel: 0844 335 1802
Luton, tel: 01582 405 100
Stansted, tel: 0870 000 0303
London City, tel: 020 7646 0088

Arrival by train

Eurostar services from Paris Gare du Nord take around 2¼ hours (Paris, tel: +33 8 92 35 35 39), and from Brussels 2 hours (Brussels, tel: +32 70 79 79 89) to the terminal at London St Pancras. For UK bookings, tel: 03432 186 186; for bookings from abroad +44 1233 617 575. Also visit www.eurostar.com.

Vehicles are also carried by **Le Shuttle** trains through the tunnel between Folkestone in Kent and Sangatte in France. There are two to five departures each hour, and the trip takes 35 minutes. Bookings are not essential, but advisable at peak times. Fares vary according to the time of travel and how far in advance you book: late at night or early morning are usually cheaper. For information and reservations tel: 08443 353 535 (UK), 0810 63 03 04 (France) or from any other country 00 33 (0)3 2100 2061, or visit www.euro tunnel.com.

C

CLIMATE

London's climate is generally mild all year round. Snow is unusual, and January temperatures average 6°C (43°F). Temperatures in the summer months average 18°C (64°F), but they can soar, causing the city to become very stuffy. It often rains, so keep an umbrella handy at all times.

CYCLING

Cycling in London can be intimidating, but a bike is often the quickest means of getting around the city. Extensive information on cycling in London can be found on the Transport for London website, www.tfl.gov.uk, which has information on the Santander Cycles hire scheme (found all over the city). You can pay at docking stations with a credit or debit card. More information is available from the London Cycle Network (www.londoncyclenetwork. org.uk) and the London Cycling Campaign (www.lcc.org.uk). A new network of cycle lanes, Cycle Super-highways, are being developed to run from outer London into and across central London. Check http://tfl.gov. uk for the latest routes.

D

DISABLED ACCESS

Artsline (www.artsline.org.uk), London's information and advice service on disability access to arts and entertainment events, provides detailed access information for venues across London, including theatres, cinemas, museums, arts centres, tourist attractions, comedy and music venues, and selected restaurants. DisabledGo (www.disabledgo.com) is a good website for facilities throughout the UK. For details on public transport pick up *Access to the Underground* (free from ticket offices) and Transport for London's *Transport Accessibility* (http:// tfl.gov.uk/transport-accessibility). Artsline is a free telephone and online information service for disabled people in London, covering the arts and entertainment.

DRIVING

Unless you are planning on making
several trips outside the capital, a car
is most likely to be more of a hindrance
than a help, and certainly a consider-
able expense, owing to the congestion
charge and the high cost of parking. If
you are driving, be sure to observe the
speed limits (police detection cameras
are increasingly common).

Congestion charge: Cars driving
into a clearly marked Congestion
Zone, extending between Kensington
and the City, between 7am and 6pm
Mon–Fri are filmed, and their drivers
are fined if a payment of £11.50 has
not been made by midnight the same
day (or £14 the following day). You can
pay at many small shops, including
newsagents, by phone (tel: 0345 900
1234) or at www.cclondon.com.

Parking: This is a big problem in
congested central London. Meters
are slightly less expensive than NCP
(multistorey) car parks, but some only
allow parking for a maximum of two
hours; it can also be hard to find a free
one. Most meter parking is free after
6.30pm daily, after 1.30pm in most
areas on Saturday, and all day Sunday,
but always check this on the meter.

E

EMBASSIES

Australia: Australia House, Strand,
WC2B 4LA; tel: 020 7379 4334
Canada: Canada House, Trafalgar
Square, SW1Y 5BJ. Tel: 020 7004 6000
Ireland: 17 Grosvenor Place, SW1X
7HR; tel: 020 7235 2171

New Zealand: 80 Haymarket, SW1Y
4TQ; tel: 020 7930 8422
US: 24 Grosvenor Square, W1A 1AE;
tel: 020 7499 9000

EMERGENCIES

For police, fire brigade or ambulance
dial 999 from any telephone (no
money or card required) and tell the
operator which service you require.

G

GAY AND LESBIAN

With Europe's largest gay and lesbian
population, London has an abundance
of bars, restaurants and clubs to
cater for most tastes, with the scene
focusing around Soho, Earl's Court
and Vauxhall. For listings, consult
the free gay weekly magazines, *Boyz*
and *QX*. Monthly magazines for sale
include *Gay Times*, *Diva* and *Attitude*.

Useful telephone contacts for advice and counselling include Switchboard, the LGBT+ helpline – previously
known as the London Lesbian and Gay
Switchboard – (10am–11pm daily; tel:
0300 330 0630; http://switchboard.
lgbt) and London Friend (7.30–9.30pm
Mon–Wed; tel: 020 7837 3337).

H

HEALTH AND MEDICAL CARE

EU citizens can receive free treatment
on producing a European Health
Insurance Card; citizens of other
countries must pay, except for emergency treatment (always free). Major
hospitals include:

Charing Cross Hospital (Fulham Palace Road, W6; tel: 020 8846 1234), University College London Hospitals (switchboard tel 020 020 3456 7890) and St Thomas's (Lambeth Palace Road, SE1; tel: 020 7188 7188). Guy's Hospital Dental Department is at St Thomas Street, SE1; tel: as before 020 7188 7188. For the nearest hospital or doctor's, or for non-life-threating medical advice ring NHS Direct, tel: 111. Late pharmacy: Bliss Chemist, 5 Marble Arch, W1, opens till midnight.

I

INTERNET

Free Wi-Fi internet access is increasingly common in London, in coffee shops, hotels, pubs and bookstores. Pay-as-you-go internet access is available at many internet cafés.

L

LEFT LUGGAGE

Most of the capital's main railway stations have left-luggage departments where you can leave your suitcases on a short-term basis, although all are extremely sensitive to potential terrorist bombs. Left-luggage offices close at around 10pm (including St Pancras) or 11pm, with the exception of Victoria, which remains open until midnight.

LOST PROPERTY

For possessions lost on public transport or in taxis, contact Transport for London's central Lost Property, 200 Baker Street, NW1 5RZ (tel: 0343 222 1234; www.tfl.gov.uk/lostproperty), Mon–Fri 8.30am–4pm, or fill in an enquiry form, available from any London Underground station or bus garage. If you lose your passport, let your embassy know as well as the nearest police station (check http://content. met.police.uk for the location and number of your nearest local station).

M

MAPS

For detailed exploration of the city centre and suburbs, the London *A–Z* books, with all roads indexed, come in various formats. Free tube maps are available at Underground stations.

MONEY

Banks: These usually open 9.30am–4.30/5pm Monday to Friday, with Saturday-morning banking common in shopping areas. Major English banks tend to offer similar exchange rates, so it is only worth looking around if you have large amounts of money to change. Currency exchange is offered at main post office branches and is commission free.

ATMs: The easiest way to take out currency is using an ATM. There are myriad cash machines across London, inside and outside banks, in supermarkets and at rail and tube stations. They operate on global credit and debit systems including Maestro/Cirrus, Switch, Visa and others.

Credit cards: International credit cards are almost universally accepted in shops, restaurants, hotels etc.

MUSEUMS AND GALLERIES

Although national museums and galleries are free, most others have entrance charges. The **London Pass** (tel: 01664 485 020; www.londonpass.com) allows free entry to several dozen attractions plus free travel on the tube and buses.

Joining the Art Fund (0844 415 4100; www.artfund.org) costs around £46 a year and provides free admission to over 200 museums, galleries and historic houses around the country, plus discounts on some exhibitions.

N

NEWSPAPERS AND LISTINGS

Daily national papers include the *Daily Telegraph* and *The Times* (both on the right politically), *The Independent* (in the middle; online only) and *The Guardian* (left of centre). Most have Sunday equivalents. The *Financial Times* is more business and finance orientated. Except for the *Daily Mirror*, the tabloids (*The Sun, Star, Daily Mail, Daily Express* and *Metro*) are right-wing.

The free *Evening Standard* and Metro (Mon–Fri), given away at stations, are good for cinema and theatre listings. For the most comprehensive, up-to-the-minute listings go to www.timeout.com/london.

P

POSTAL SERVICES

Most post offices open Mon–Fri 9am–5pm, Sat 9am–noon. London's main post office (24–8 William IV Street; Mon, Wed–Fri 8.30am–6.30pm, Tue open from 9.15am, Sat 9am–5.30pm) is by Trafalgar Square, behind the church of St-Martin-in-the-Fields.

POSTCODES

The first half of London postcodes indicates the general area (WC = West Central, SE = South East) and the second half, used only for mail, identifies the exact block. Here is a key to some of the commoner codes:

W1 Mayfair, Marylebone, Soho; W2 Bayswater; W4 Chiswick; W8 Kensington; W11 Notting Hill; WC1 Bloomsbury; WC2 Covent Garden, Strand; E1 Whitechapel; EC1 Clerkenwell; EC2 Bank, Barbican; EC4 St Paul's, Blackfriars; SW1 St James's, Belgravia; SW3 Chelsea; SW7 Knightsbridge, South Kensington; SW19 Wimbledon; SE1 Lambeth, Southwark; SE10 Greenwich; SE21 Dulwich; N1 Hoxton, Islington; N6 Highgate; NW3 Hampstead.

PUBLIC HOLIDAYS

1 Jan: New Year's Day
Mar/Apr: Good Fri; Easter Mon
May: May Day (first Mon of month); Spring Bank Holiday (last Mon)
Aug: Summer Bank Holiday (last Mon of month)
25 Dec: Christmas Day
26 Dec: Boxing Day

PUBLIC TRANSPORT

Tickets and fares

London's transport map is divided into six zones, spreading outwards from central London (zones 1–2) to cover all of Greater London. Tube and rail fares are priced according to which zones you travel in. Single tickets on London's transport networks are very expensive, so it's best to buy one of several multi-journey passes. **Travel cards** give unlimited travel on the tube, buses and DLR. Off-peak travel cards (valid after 9.30am) are considerably cheaper. You can also buy three-day or seven-day cards along with a London Pass.

Oyster cards are smart cards that you charge up with credit (using cash or a credit card), then touch in on card readers at tube stations, buses and some railway stations (see Rail), so that an amount is deducted each time you use it. They are cheaper than travel cards if you only expect to travel a few times each day. Cards and Oysters can be bought from tube and DLR stations and newsagents. Visitors can order them ahead from www.visitbritaindirect.com. You can also use a contactless debit card in the same way, and the same price for a single fare, as an Oyster card.

Under-11s travel free on the tube and DLR at off-peak times provided they are with an adult. Otherwise, Travelcards for children aged 5–15 are available at a special reduced rate. Children under 16 travel for free at all times on buses, but 14- to 15-year-olds need a 14–15 Oyster photocard.

For full details of all fares, see www.tfl.gov.uk.

Underground (tube)

The fastest and easiest way to get around London is by tube. Try to avoid the rush hours (8am–9.30am and 5–6.30pm), when trains are packed

with commuters. Services run from 5.30am to just after midnight. Make sure you have a ticket and keep hold of it after you have passed through the barrier; you will need it to exit. Oyster cards are a wise buy if you plan to travel a lot by tube. For enquiries, tel: 0343 222 1234; www.tfl.gov.uk.

Docklands Light Railway

The DLR runs from Bank and Tower Gateway to east and southeast London destinations. Tickets are the same type and cost as for the tube.

Rail

London's commuter rail network provides links to areas not on underground lines. Travelcards are still valid on rail services for journeys within the correct zones. Oyster cards and your UK contactless debit card can only be used on London Overground stations. These are the principal mainline stations, with the areas of London and the rest of the country they serve:

Charing Cross Station. Services to south London and southeast England: Canterbury, Folkestone, Hastings, Dover Priory.

Euston Station. Services to northwest London and beyond to Birmingham and the northwest: Liverpool, Manchester, Glasgow.

King's Cross Station. Services to north London and beyond to the northeast: Leeds, York, Newcastle, Edinburgh and Aberdeen.

St Pancras Station. The Eurostar terminal for trains from Paris and Brussels, plus fast trains east to Kent, including

Canterbury and Margate, plus some destinations in the East Midlands.

Liverpool Street Station and **Fenchurch Street**. To east and northeast London, Cambridge and East Anglia.

Paddington Station. Services to west London and to Oxford, Bath, Bristol, the west, and South Wales.

Victoria Station. Services to south London and southeast England, including Gatwick Airport, Brighton, Newhaven and Dover.

Waterloo Station. To southwest London, Southampton, and southern England as far as Exeter, including Richmond, Windsor and Ascot.

Other terminals, such as **Marylebone**, **London Bridge**, **Cannon Street** and **Blackfriars**, are mainly commuter stations, used for destinations around London.

Thameslink services run through the city centre, while the **London Overground** connects Richmond to Stratford, via the north of the capital, and Dalston Junction to West Croydon – connecting southeast to northeast London on the East London line.

For times and enquiries; tel: 0845 748 4950; www.nationalrail.co.uk.

Bus

If you are not in a hurry, travel by bus provides a good way of seeing London; the bus network is very comprehensive. You cannot pay by cash or paper tickets – use an Oyster, contactless debit card, a travel card or a one-day bus pass. Again, an Oyster card is the best bet, as each journey then costs £1.50, and the total is price-capped at £4.50 per day.

Night buses run all night on the most popular routes, approximately every 30 minutes. Full bus route maps are available at Travel Information Centres.

Boat

River cruises are a great way to see London's sights, and various routes run on the Thames between Hampton Court and Barrier Gardens. There is a hop-on-hop-off River Rover pass; see www.citycruises.com.

T

TAXIS

Black cabs are licensed and display the charges on the meter. They can be hailed in the street if their 'for hire' sign is lit. There are also ranks at major train stations and at various points across the city, or you can order a cab on 0871 871 8710. Black cabs are licensed to carry up to five people (six in the special Metrocabs and Mercedes Vitos) plus luggage. There are no additional charges for extra passengers or items of luggage within these limits. All black cabs are wheelchair accessible.

There is an additional charge when you take a black cab from Heathrow Airport and when you book a black cab by telephone. Many black cabs accept payment by credit or debit card (for an additional charge), but check with the driver before the trip starts.

You can tip taxi drivers as much as you like, but most people round up to the nearest pound.

Minicabs should only be hired by phone; they are not allowed to pick up passengers on the street. Reputable firms include: Addison Lee, tel: 020 7387 8888; www.addisonlee.com.

TELEPHONES

London's UK dialling code is 020. To call from abroad, dial '44', the international access code for Britain, then 20 (the London code, with the initial '0' dropped), then the individual number. London 8-digit numbers then begin with 7, 8 or – a recent new number – 3.

Useful numbers

Emergency – police, fire, ambulance: tel: 999
Operator (for difficulties in getting through): tel: 100
International Operator: tel: 155
Directory Enquiries (UK): tel: 118 500 or 118 888 or 118 811 (calls are expensive to these numbers)
International Directory Enquiries: tel: 118 505 or 118 866 or 118 899

THEATRE TICKETS

The only way to get a ticket at face value is to buy it from the theatre box office. Most open 10am–mid-evening. You can pay by credit card over the phone for most theatres, or reserve seats three days in advance before paying. A ticket booth (TKTS) on the south side of Leicester Square offers unsold seats at half price or three–quarter price (plus booking fee) on the day of performance (Mon–Sat 10am–7pm, Sun 11am–4.30pm). Two reputable agents are Ticketmaster (www.ticketmaster.co.uk) and See Tickets (www.seetickets.com).

TIME

In winter, Great Britain is on Greenwich Mean Time, which is 8 hours ahead of Los Angeles, 5 hours ahead of New York and Montreal, and 10 hours behind Sydney. During the summer, from the last Sunday in March to the last Sunday in October, clocks are put forward one hour.

TOURIST OFFICES

The official tourist board (www.visit london.com) offers information on sights, events and practical points, plus a commercial hotel booking service. Personal enquiries can be made at Britain and London Visitor Centre, 1 Regent Street, Piccadilly Circus, SW1Y 4XT (Mon 9.30am–6.30pm, Tue–Fri 9am–6.30pm, Sat–Sun 10am–4pm, except June–Sept Sat 9am–5pm).

There are other tourist information centres in the City (St Paul's Churchyard; tel: 020 7332 1456) and Greenwich (Pepys House, 2 Cutty Sark Gardens; tel: 0870 608 2000).

WEBSITES

In addition to the many websites listed in this guidebook, the following are useful for information on London:
www.bbc.co.uk/london (BBC London)
www.standard.co.uk (*Evening Standard* site; useful listings)
www.metro.co.uk (*Metro* newspaper)
www.timeout.com/london (for up-to-the-minute news, listings and reviews on cultural events across the capital).

INDEX

Tube map

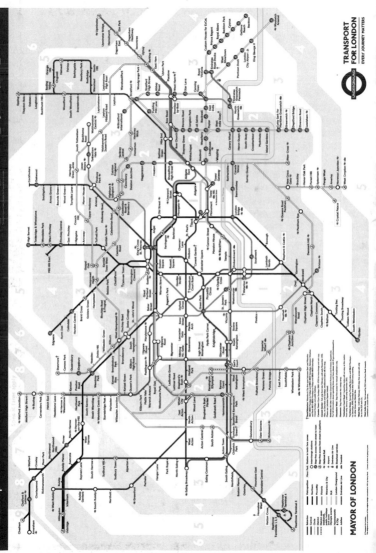

tfl.gov.uk
i 24 hour travel information 0343 222 1234*
Sign up for email updates tfl.gov.uk/emailupdates
@TfLTravelAlerts

TRANSPORT
FOR LONDON
EVERY JOURNEY MATTERS

UNDERGROUND

MAYOR OF LONDON

Experience London
Editor: Carine Tracanelli
Author: Bridget Freer, Emma Levine
Head of Production: Rebeka Davies
Picture Editor: Tom Smyth
Cartography: original cartography Apa
Publications, updated by Carte
Photography: 4Corners Images 12; Alamy
16B, 35, 52, 59, 104, 113, 127, 140/141;
Anthony Webb/REX/Shutterstock 139; David
Loftus/Corbin & King 28; Dean and Chapter
of Westminster 77; Depositphotos 43; Geo.
F. Trumper 36; Getty Images 1, 14, 29, 31,
37, 38/39, 41, 54, 56, 61, 69, 71, 75, 76, 82,
85, 92, 95, 105, 108, 118, 130, 138, 142, 143,
146, 157; Historic Royal Palaces 73; iStock
60, 70; John Tramper 125; Jon Arnold/AWL
Images 4/5; Jorge Royan 94; Lisa Linder
137; Lydia Evans/Apa Publications 6, 8, 10,
13, 15T, 15B, 18, 19B, 21, 24, 30, 33, 40, 44,
49, 55, 58, 62, 72, 74, 78, 83, 86, 88/89, 90,
91, 93, 96, 107, 111, 114, 122, 126, 128/129,
131, 132, 145, 149, 150, 154, 155, 160, 161,
162/163; Mandarin Oriental Hotel Group
148; Maybourne Hotels 16T, 147; Miles Willis
158/159; Ming Tang-Evans/Apa Publications
19T, 32, 50, 51, 66, 67, 68, 112, 119, 124,
136, 156; Museum of London 110; Public
domain 57; Rhubarb 106; ROH 11; Shangri-
La International 120/121; Shutterstock 17,
100, 123, 144; Sir John Soane's Museum 87;
Stefan Johnson 9, 102/103; SuperStock 109;
The Connaught 34, 42; The Royal Exchange
101; TopFoto 53
Cover: Getty Images

Distribution
UK, Ireland and Europe
Apa Publications (UK) Ltd
sales@insightguides.com
United States and Canada
Ingram Publisher Services
ips@ingramcontent.com
Australia and New Zealand
Woodslane
info@woodslane.com.au

Southeast Asia
Apa Publications (SN) Pte;
singaporeoffice@insightguides.com
Hong Kong, Taiwan and China
Apa Publications (HK) Ltd
hongkongoffice@insightguides.com
Worldwide
Apa Publications (UK) Ltd
sales@insightguides.com

**Special Sales, Content Licensing
and CoPublishing**
Insight Guides can be purchased in bulk
quantities at discounted prices. We can create
special editions, personalised jackets and
corporate imprints tailored to your needs.
sales@insightguides.com
www.insightguides.biz

First Edition 2016

All Rights Reserved
© 2016 Apa Digital (CH) AG and Apa
Publications (UK) Ltd

Printed in China by CTPS

Contact us
Every effort has been made to provide
accurate information in this publication,
but changes are inevitable. The publisher
cannot be responsible for any resulting loss,
inconvenience or injury. We would appreciate
it if readers would call our attention to any
errors or outdated information. We also
welcome your suggestions; please contact us
at: hello@insightguides.com
www.insightguides.com